Praise for *Passion Pursuit*

W9-CLH-830

Let's face it, a Bible study on this topic is long overdue. Sex and passion in marriage are topics often addressed only on the surface level in our friendships and even in our churches. In *Passion Pursuit*, Juli and Linda have chosen to dive deeply, answering real women's questions—even the ones we are often too afraid to ask. The combined wisdom and integrity of these two women, coupled with their refusal to avoid even the most intimate issues, will have this resource flying off bookshelves and into the hands and hearts of women who want real passion in their marriage. Every wife, everywhere, needs to do this Bible study. It will change the most important relationship in her life.

PRISCILLA SHIRER
Teacher and author

Juli Slattery and Linda Dillow have joined together to address some of the deepest sexual questions, struggles, and wounds of our era. It is a rare gift to the body of Christ for their remarkable wisdom, depth of experience, and passion for Jesus to be united to offer hope and direction. What they will bring us to enliven our passion and intensify our holiness will be a remarkable kingdom labor.

DAN B. ALLENDER, PHD
Professor of Counseling Psychology and founding president,
The Seattle School of Theology and Psychology

It's about time! This powerful resource is long overdue and incredibly helpful. And who better to do it than Linda Dillow and Juli Slattery. *Passion Pursuit* is biblically grounded, immeasurably helpful, and desperately needed. You will love it!

DRS. LES AND LESLIE PARROTT
LesAndLeslie.com, authors of *Love Talk*

Do you long for that spark to return to your marriage, long to see your passions reignited? It's not only possible, it's God's plan and deep desire for you! Linda Dillow and Dr. Juli Slattery have provided a treasure map to help you lay hold of God's best design for passion and intimacy with your husband. You're about to embark on an adventure that will challenge, heal, and establish you beyond your wildest dreams. Don't settle for less than God's absolute best for you. Learn from these dear friends of mine. They are seasoned, wise, women of God.

SUSIE LARSON
Author, speaker, radio host

Passion Pursuit gently yet unapologetically leads Christian women to that most marvelous of places: helping them to care about their sexual relationship as much as God does. Women who go through this fine study will certainly feel themselves drawing not just closer to their husbands but also closer to God. Not only will they find themselves more pleasing to their husbands and more capable of experiencing greater personal delight themselves, but along the way they will also be led to become more and more like Christ. A marvelous aim, successfully achieved and brilliantly executed.

GARY THOMAS
Author of *Sacred Marriage* and *The Sacred Search*

Passion Pursuit: What Kind of Love Are You Making? is a bold, holy, and incredibly needed study. With gentle and godly candor, Linda and Juli invite women to pursue the healing and delight God intends for husbands and wives to enjoy. Linda's and Juli's wisdom and love for Jesus permeates every page and sheds light on a subject that for too many women has been shrouded by darkness. There is a great good to be discovered here!

STASI ELDREDGE
Author, *Becoming Myself* and coauthor of *Captivating* and *Love and War*

Juli and Linda are stepping into a whole new area of Bible study for women—intimacy in marriage. It is a topic that has been ignored long enough. They absolutely lead, bless, and encourage women into a deeper relationship with the Lord and their husbands. Together, they bring a unique and fun approach to a topic that many couples struggle with in marriage. By the end of the study, many women will have found new freedom and recognition of the amazing gift God has given them in their marriage. *Passion Pursuit* is a home run!

DR. GREG AND ERIN SMALLEY
Fight Your Way to a Better Marriage
www.smalleymarriage.com

Linda and Juli offer biblically sound teaching interspersed with personal insights that are both wise and whimsical. This workbook isn't two authors spouting their own philosophies—it's two friends gently guiding you through the Scriptures and posing questions that are sure to inspire fresh ideas about your sexuality and how you view intimacy.

LORRAINE PINTUS
author of *Jump Off the Hormone Swing* and coauthor of *Intimate Issues*

Sex is a hot topic. But for many women, sex is uncomfortable, an obligation, or a reminder of past hurts. Linda Dillow and Dr. Juli Slattery encourage women about a subject that is often not discussed. *Passion Pursuit* is a Bible study that is relevant, informative, and sensitive to the questions that many women want answered but don't know who to ask. Together the authors address the subject with transparency about their own lives, information from research, and spiritual application from Scripture.

Passion Pursuit is a resource for every woman who wants God's best out of life and marriage!

DEBBIE ALSDORF
Author of *A Woman Who Trusts God*

This is one of the most important Bible studies a church can offer to married women. Juli and Linda tackle difficult topics with solid truth and a refreshing lightness. The answers the church has failed to provide about sex and intimacy can be found right here.

DANNAH GRESH
Bestselling author of *And the Bride Wore White* and *Get Lost*

A dynamic duo, Linda Dillow and Juli Slattery team up to show women how to put the sizzle back in their marriages. With transparency, wisdom, and at times, humor, Linda and Juli speak directly to women's hearts about pursuing passion in their marriages. If you don't want your marriage to become boring, this is a must read!

BECKY HARLING
International author and speaker
Freedom from Performing: Grace in an Applause-Driven World

You mean Christian women can, do, and should enjoy sex? Whodathunkit? Well, God did—first; but then all sorts of well-meaning experts created a mess with all things Christian+sex+
female+marriage+fun+healthy. As such, it's been difficult to find a book that engagingly couples biblical counsel with wise, funny, relatable, and thoroughly modern discussion—but Linda Dillow and Dr. Juli Slattery have accomplished just that! I highly recommend *Passion Pursuit*'s spiritually saucy pages to every woman of faith. After all, satisfying, fun, and guilt-free sex was God's idea from the very beginning.

JULIE BARNHILL
National and international speaker, author of ten books

While the world fixates on sex, the church has remained silent, and this has led to much confusion and pain in the Christian community. Now finally Dr. Juli Slattery and Linda Dillow have boldly stepped out and addressed the issues in a biblical, clear, and courageous way. *Passion Pursuit* opens the door to much healing, much pleasure, and much clarity on the sexual experience. It offers a more beautiful, passionate, and pleasurable picture for both husband and wife than the world can ever give. It will drastically change marriages and heal broken hearts. I pray every church in America will embrace this study for their women—and do so quickly!

PAT HARLEY
Teacher and speaker, *The Amazing Collection*
President, Big Dream Ministries

If you are looking for excellence in a study, then stop looking—the book you're holding is the most valuable book on the market! Gary and I have written and read many but Juli and Linda's study on passion is at the top of our list!

DR. GARY AND BARB ROSBERG
6 Secrets to a Lasting Love

Every married woman needs to study *Passion Pursuit*. Marriage is foundational to families, children, and the shaping of the next generation of adults. This book inspires, instructs, gives hope and grace plus shows how to embrace marriage wholeheartedly as one of the best works of a woman's life.

SALLY CLARKSON
Popular conference speaker, blogger (itakejoy.com), and author of seven books, including *Desperate: Hope for the Mom Who Needs to Breathe*

Linda and Juli are two wise women who share with candor and grace about true intimacy in marriage. *Passion Pursuit* will bring up areas in your intimate life that have the potential to lead you to freedom if you are willing to "go there." I highly recommend you read this book with a friend or a mentor so you can discuss, confess, and find healing as you pursue passion in your marriage.

SARAH MAE
coauthor of *Desperate: Hope for the Mom Who Needs to Breathe*

PASSION PURSUIT

What Kind of Love Are You Making?

Linda Dillow

Dr. Juli Slattery

MOODY PUBLISHERS

CHICAGO

All Scripture quotations, unless otherwise indicated, are taken from the Holy Bible, New International Version®, NIV®. Copyright ©1973, 1978, 1984 by Biblica, Inc.™ Used by permission of Zondervan. All rights reserved worldwide.

Scripture quotations marked NASB are taken from the *New American Standard Bible®*, Copyright © 1960, 1962, 1963, 1968, 1971, 1972, 1973, 1975, 1977, 1995 by The Lockman Foundation. Used by permission. (www.Lockman.org)

Scripture quotations marked THE MESSAGE are from *The Message,* copyright © by Eugene H. Peterson 1993, 1994, 1995. Used by permission of NavPress Publishing Group.

Scripture quotations marked NLT are taken from the *Holy Bible, New Living Translation,* copyright © 1996, 2004. Used by permission of Tyndale House Publishers, Inc., Wheaton, Illinois 60189, U.S.A. All rights reserved.

Scripture quotations marked AMP are taken from *The Amplified Bible.* Copyright © 1965, 1987 by The Zondervan Corporation. *The Amplified New Testament* copyright © 1958, 1987 by The Lockman Foundation. Used by permission.

Edited by Terry Behimer
Interior and cover design: www.DesignByJulia
Illustrations: Julia Ryan / www.DesignByJulia
Cover images: photos © Shutterstock.com Stephen Coburn / Ally London. Illustration: Julia Ryan
Interior photos: © Shutterstock.com
Photos of authors: Cathy Walters Photography

Library of Congress Cataloging-in-Publication Data

Dillow, Linda.
  Passion pursuit : what kind of love are you making? / Linda Dillow, Dr. Juli Slattery.
    pages cm
  Includes bibliographical references.
  ISBN 978-0-8024-0639-2
  1. Sex--Religious aspects--Christianity--Textbooks. 2. Intimacy (Psychology)--Religious aspects--Christianity--Textbooks. 3. Wives--Sexual behavior--Textbooks. I. Title.
  BT708.D543 2013
  248.8'435--dc23

2013001061

We hope you enjoy this book from Moody Publishers. Our goal is to provide high-quality, thought-provoking books and products that connect truth to your real needs and challenges. For more information on other books and products written and produced from a biblical perspective, go to www.moodypublishers.com or write to:

Moody Publishers
820 N. LaSalle Boulevard
Chicago, IL 60610

1 3 5 7 9 10 8 6 4 2

Printed in the United States of America

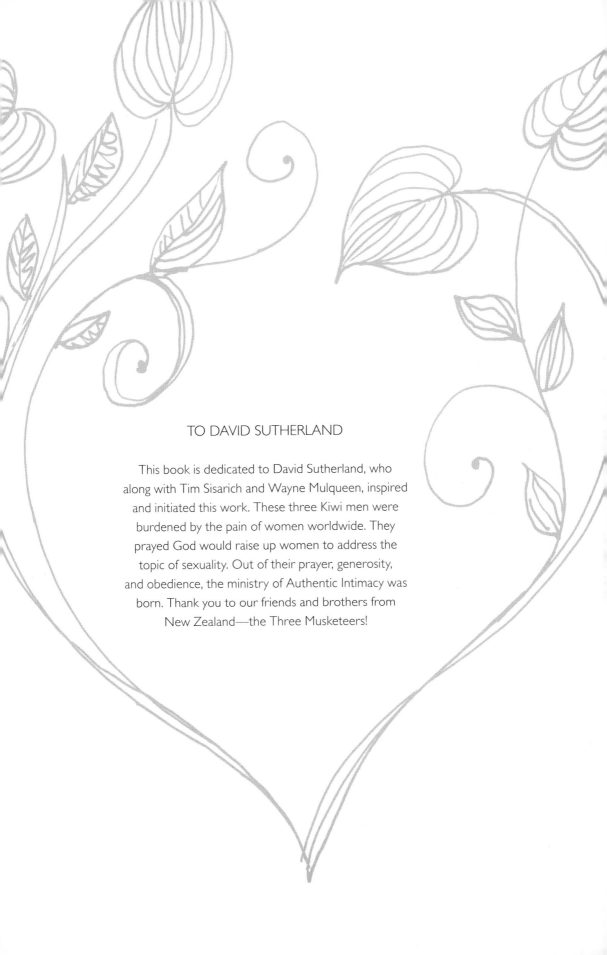

TO DAVID SUTHERLAND

This book is dedicated to David Sutherland, who along with Tim Sisarich and Wayne Mulqueen, inspired and initiated this work. These three Kiwi men were burdened by the pain of women worldwide. They prayed God would raise up women to address the topic of sexuality. Out of their prayer, generosity, and obedience, the ministry of Authentic Intimacy was born. Thank you to our friends and brothers from New Zealand—the Three Musketeers!

A Personal Note to You / 10

Chapter 1.   I've Got Power 12

Chapter 2.   Me, Pursue Passion? 31

Chapter 3.   God's Got an Opinion! 47

Chapter 4.   Making Truth Stick 62

Chapter 5.   What Kind of Love Are You Making? 78

Chapter 6.   Pursuing Pure Pleasure 96

Chapter 7.   Exposing Counterfeit Intimacy 115

Chapter 8.   Debt-Free Intimacy 135

Chapter 9.   The Passion Priority 154

Chapter 10. Becoming a Smokin' Hot Mama 172

Notes / 188

Acknowledgments / 190

Discussion Guidelines / 191

A Personal Note to You

Dear Friend,

We feel like we will quickly become friends because this is a unique Bible study. We will be sharing very personally with you and asking you to search some deep things in your life with the Lord. Although we haven't met you, we have prayed for you. We have asked the Lord to give us words that will minister directly to your heart.

As we address the subject of intimacy in your marriage, we believe you will enjoy many "aha" moments in these next ten weeks. We anticipate you will discover more freedom and fun in your intimate relationship with your husband and that you'll gain new insights about how your sexuality and spirituality flow together. But rest assured of this—we won't sidestep sensitive topics. We'll hit head-on your deep questions and address your concerns with honesty, humor, and most importantly, the truth of God's Word.

We are from two different generations but we have the same heart. We both love God's Word and believe the answers to life and intimacy in marriage are hidden in its pages. We have wrestled through how to apply the timeless truths of God to our own lives and we've been privileged to walk alongside many women through their marriage journeys.

This workbook has an accompanying DVD series that has lots of additional teaching and stories. If you are watching those sessions, then you've already gotten to know us but we want to share a bit more about our lives.

Linda: Let me paint a picture of my very special friend Juli. Imagine a petite forty-four-year-old with a ninety-year-old wise saint stuck inside her. Juli is the Energizer Bunny on steroids with a Bible in one hand and A Guide to Psychotherapy in the other. Her lips utter brilliant exegesis of Scripture, yet a mischievous pixie peers out from behind her sparkling brown eyes. Juli's favorite shoes are Nikes, because when she's not climbing a mountain, she is chasing her three wonderful boys or working out with Mike, her husband of nineteen years. I am old enough to be Juli's mom, and yet God has graced me with her friendship and partnership in this exciting project. Juli has an intimate walk with her Father God, and it is such a joy to fall to our knees together and seek God's wisdom for you—a wife He loves.

Juli: Linda is one of the most incredible women I have ever met. She's fun, spunky, and you just never know what will come out of her mouth. Likely it's something that bends you over in hysterics or a snatch of wisdom that stops you in your tracks. She's been married to Jody for forty-nine years, and they have four grown kids and ten grandkids.

For seventeen years, Jody and Linda lived in Europe and Asia as missionaries. Yes, I agree, it's a little freaky to think of a grandmother/ missionary who teaches on sex, but believe me, Linda goes way beyond teaching the "missionary position." This woman is fearless in addressing the most intimate questions, yet her words on this sensitive topic are always seasoned with compassion, grace, and wisdom. What makes Linda most unique is her special friendship with Jesus. You can't spend time with her without recognizing that her words and actions are a reflection of the Lord.

What's in This for You?

Even if you are a veteran of Bible studies or women's groups, one on sexual intimacy may be a little bit intimidating. After all, it's not a topic that is openly addressed in most church settings. As part of a small group, or even if you're doing this study alone or with a friend, we suggest you take a moment to review the guidelines on page 191. Sexual intimacy is a delicate and discreet subject that must be approached with candor yet sensitivity. We have prayed that the Lord would give us the wisdom to strike this balance in Passion Pursuit. We are committed to addressing your most intimate and pressing questions but doing so within the framework of authenticity, sensitivity, and respect. And we will even have some fun!

God wants to do a mighty work in your marriage. His desire is to reclaim and rebuild the beautiful gift of sexuality. We understand that you and other women taking this course come from many different walks of life. You will meet some who are looking for encouragement for an already strong marriage. Others are desperate for the hope of intimacy to be rekindled. Still others will be limping with deep wounds from past sexual abuse or broken trust. Whatever desires and heartaches you personally are bringing with you to this study, we want you to know that the Lord cares deeply for you. His truth is able to bring hope and healing as you pursue passion for Him and your husband.

This is our prayer for you personally:

Abba Father,

Take your daughter by the hand and tenderly teach her exactly what You know she needs so that she may experience the freedom to pursue passion in her marriage. Where healing is needed, let her know You as Healer. When she needs encouragement, be her Encourager. Let her know that on each step of this journey, You are holding her with Your love.

"Now to him who is able to do immeasurably more than all we ask or imagine, according to his power that is at work within us, to him be glory in the church and in Christ Jesus throughout all generations, for ever and ever! Amen" (Ephesians 3:20–21).

Your new friends,

Linda   Jul

Note of caution: Passion Pursuit is not for every woman. The principles we will be exploring throughout this study apply to relatively healthy marriages. Most couples struggle through problems with communication difficulties, misunderstanding, selfishness, sexual temptation, and mistakes from the past. However, if your marriage involves deeper issues like domestic violence, homosexuality, or addictions, you need to seek help from a pastor and/or a mental health professional. You may also find that while studying Passion Pursuit, wounds from the past are reopened. We believe this is part of God's healing journey for you. But you may need additional support as you invite God to redeem your past. Please visit us at www. authenticintimacy.com for additional resources.

I've Got Power

A Bible study on sex for women.
Now, that's different.

We've got news for you—God cares about sex. He created it. And He cares about your intimate relationship with your husband. He cares deeply about your heart and the wounds you may have been carrying around for many years.

Why study what He has to say about sex?
Because Jesus is the Healer.
He is your Redeemer.
He is the One who restores.
Your God is able to overcome any barrier.

We know that you have barriers in your marriage. We have had them too and have learned to study God's truth and fall upon His grace in the midst of it all. So buckle up as we dive into *Passion Pursuit*.

When I Began to Pursue Passion

When I (Juli) had been married about ten years, I noticed that intimacy in my marriage had become, well, boring. In fact, I was so bored with the "same old" intimacy that I calculated in my mind approximately how many times my husband and I had probably done the same thing. I figured that, if we had sex on average twice a week, that was about 100 times a year or 1,000 times over ten years of marriage. Yeah, I know. Who thinks like that? The next thought I had was, *Something's gotta change. My bedroom ceiling just isn't that fascinating!*

That little mental exercise was a wake-up call for me. I wanted sexual intimacy in my marriage to be fun, new, and creative. If sex was dull after ten years, how would I feel after thirty years of marriage?

CHAPTER ONE

THEME:

You have power, the power to build a house of intimacy by God's design.

THEME VERSE:

"The wise woman builds her house, but with her own hands the foolish one tears hers down."
(Proverbs 14:1)

Regardless of where your marriage is, it's time for a wake-up call. Passion doesn't just happen—it must be pursued, sought after, and longed for. Unfortunately, most marriages get stuck when it comes to passion, romance, intimacy.

Pain simmered in Karin's eyes:

Sex is so overrated. What is the big deal anyway? Passion walked out our bedroom door with the first baby and has never returned. Making love has become, "You touch me here, I touch you there, you move inside me, and it's over before it's begun." And that is supposed to make me feel close to my husband? There are nights that I cry myself to sleep, drowning in isolation while he slumbers in a distant land right next to me.

Joy danced in Shannon's eyes:

Our intimate oneness grows deeper, better, more fun every year. Sex is where we escape from life and delight in the gift of each other. The intimacy we share, the exquisite pleasure we give, brings such joy. We can leave our hiding place of love refreshed—better prepared to face kids, problems, all of real life. How I thank God for His amazing gift of sexual passion.

We rejoice with Shannon but know that many wives identify with Karin. Perhaps the most depressing feeling a woman can have is absolute helplessness to change intimacy in her marriage. Karin's words express this—she feels defeated and powerless in her loneliness.

We want you to understand that you don't need to feel powerless! God has given you power to create intimacy in your marriage. In fact, we believe that every wife is actively using her power to either build or tear down intimacy. The key is that most women don't even know they have power, and they certainly don't understand how they might be using it to destroy the oneness they long for.

Although *Passion Pursuit* is about sexual intimacy in marriage, we recognize that sexual passion was never meant to occur in a vacuum. It is intimately intertwined with emotions, security, communication, and other vital aspects of your marriage. So we want to spend our first week with you looking at the "big picture" of intimacy in marriage.

The stereotype some women have of a "Christian wife" is one of weakness—a woman who lets her husband dominate the home. Through generations, the message has been passed down that God wants women to be weak, subservient, and helpless in marriage. Newsflash: this is *not* God's design for you as a wife.

Read the theme verse, Proverbs 14:1. Does this proverb sound like one that promotes weakness in women? On the other hand, does this proverb seem to be promoting a woman dominating her husband? We believe that a key element of building intimacy in your marriage is the question of how you use your power.

Get out your highlighter because what we are about to share needs to sink to the core of your being:

A woman can make two vital mistakes that may result in the destruction of her marriage: The first is to ignore or deny her power; the second is to abuse her power.[1]

Whether through subtle or overt actions, a wife can shatter her husband's confidence and trust and sabotage his leadership ability through the misuse of her power in marriage. The philosopher Goethe expresses it well:

If you treat a man as he is, he will stay as he is. If you treat him as if he were what he ought to be and could be, he will become that bigger and better man.

We believe that within every man is a "bigger and better man." In some husbands, that hero may be emerging. In others, he may be hidden deep beneath layers of shame, anger, insecurity, or doubt. Your call as a wife is to use your abilities and influence to bring forth the bigger and better man within your husband. It is neither an easy task, nor one that will be quickly accomplished. In fact, it may take a lifetime. However, continually developing the bigger and better man in your husband is critical if you want to achieve deep intimacy and trust in your marriage.

A woman never marries the man of her dreams. She helps the man she married to become the man of his dreams.[2]

DAY 1
Your Power Zone: Respect

In building your marriage, your "power zones" directly correspond to your husband's need for respect, companionship, and sexual fulfillment. Over the next three days, we'll look at what God has to say about each of these.

Today, we want you to think specifically about your husband's need for respect and how that translates to a power zone for you. Your respect means so much to your husband because you know him in ways that no one else does. You know his weaknesses and insecurities. You've seen him fail in the past. You know his faults but by respecting him, you choose to believe in him and to focus on what is worthy of respect.

🖤 1. Let's jump right into a very familiar and important passage on marriage: Ephesians 5:33. What do God's instructions to wives in this passage say about how to use power to promote intimacy?

_____

_____

_____ ▪

Ephesians 5:33 says, "The wife must *respect* her husband." To help you understand the full meaning of the word *respect*, let's look at how *The Amplified Bible* renders this verse:

> Let the wife see that she respects and reverences her husband [that she notices him, regards him, honors him, prefers him, venerates, and esteems him; and that she defers to him, praises him, and loves and admires him exceedingly.]

You may think, "That's over the top! Surely it can't mean all that!" Oh but it does! Even now, ask God to broaden your understanding of all that respect means to your husband and how you can display respect in a way that is meaningful to him.

 2. Choose three of the words from the expanded definition of respect above and describe what they mean and what you might do to demonstrate this attribute.

_____

_____

_____

_____

_____

_____

_____

_____

_____

_____

_____

_____ ▪

I confess, I've used my power of "respect" the wrong way by comparing Mike's leadership style to that of other men. My husband is a relationship-oriented man who would rather connect with someone than drive toward a goal. Early in our marriage, I subtly criticized him for this. I felt frustrated that he didn't have ambitious career goals like men I worked with in ministry. As much as I tried to disguise my complaints as "suggestions," they eroded Mike's feelings of competence in our marriage and hurt my husband deeply. My comments were born out of my own ungrateful heart. The Lord has taught me to see and appreciate the precious ways that Mike leads me and the boys, ways that are unique to him. He is a servant leader. One of his highest "goals" is to be with me and please me. Why in the world was I complaining about that?

♥ 3. How does God's teaching to wives about respect correlate to a man's deep need to feel adequate and capable? What do you think happens to a man when he does not feel respected by his wife?

_____

_____

_____ ■

God calls us to be like Sarah, Abraham's wife. If you want to learn more about her, read Genesis 16–21. Sarah wasn't a silent or weak woman; she had opinions. However, she had a reverent attitude toward her husband—a husband who made some very BIG mistakes! In 1 Peter 3:6 we read: "You are her (Sarah's) daughters if you do what is right and do not give way to fear."

♥ 4. Read 1 Peter 3:6 and then list three fears that keep you from meeting your husband's need for respect.

_____

_____

_____ ■

♥ 5. Imagine that you have been invited to a bridal shower for a young friend. You've been asked to write a letter to this young bride about the *power of respect* in her upcoming marriage. Write your letter in the space below.

_____

_____

_____

_____

_____

_____

_____

_____ ■

♥ 6. Within the area of respect, you are either building or tearing down intimacy in your marriage. List several actions that reflect your marriage under each of the columns below:

RESPECTFUL ACTIONS THAT BUILD   DISRESPECTFUL ACTIONS THAT TEAR DOWN

_____   _____

_____   _____

_____   _____

_____   _____

_____   _____

_____   _____

_____   _____

_____   _____

_____   _____

_____   _____

_____   _____

♥ 7. What is one thing you will do in the next twenty-four hours to communicate respect to your husband?

_____

_____

_____

_____

_____

DAY 2

Your Power Zone: Companionship

Get ready to focus in on your husband's second great need—the need for companionship. Again, because companionship is a deep need in your husband, it becomes a power zone for you. God makes it very clear in Scripture that man needs a woman to be his companion. "God said, 'It's not good for the Man to be alone; I'll make him a helper, a companion'" (Genesis 2:18 MSG).

Imagine that you completely understood your husband's deep need for respect, but you stopped right there. Your entire relationship with him was built around respect. You listened to him and endorsed his every thought and decision. Is that the type of wife you want to be? The wife your husband desires? The wife God calls you to be?

While respect is vitally important, it is not your husband's only need. God created you to be your husband's friend and his trusted teammate.

The dictionary defines companionship as, "the state of being with someone." One husband said it this way: "To a man, companionship is more than just being in the same room together. Companionship is about shared space—being side by side, shared purpose—common goals or interests, and shared commitment."

So how does a woman who is convinced friendship comes through deep sharing create companionship with a husband whose view of companionship is very different? One writer said it like this:

HOW TO TREAT A WOMAN
Wine her. Dine her. Call her. Hold her. Surprise her. Compliment her. Smile at her. Listen to her. Laugh with her. Cry with her. Romance her. Encourage her. Believe in her. Pray with her. Pray for her. Cuddle with her. Shop with her. Give her jewelry. Buy her flowers. Hold her hand. Write love letters to her. Go to the ends of the earth and back again for her.

HOW TO TREAT A MAN
Show up naked. Bring chicken wings. Don't block the TV.[3]

Are we suggesting you show up naked, bring food, and don't block the TV? No . . . but we are suggesting that you remember you have power in companionship. You were designed to be your husband's trusted teammate, completer, and friend. God says friendship is a deep need in your man.

Companionship is many things. Let us share two important aspects of deep friendship.

Companionship is sharing life with your husband.

Now, you might think, *I try to share life with my husband all the time, but he's not interested.* Here's the catch—sharing life doesn't just mean talking about life. Let's put it this way: **Men like to do life together while their wives like to process life together.** What does your husband like to do? Hike? Watch movies? Golf? Build? We are *not* suggesting that you have to go hunting with your husband—although you might choose to do that. But ask yourself this question, "What activities do my husband and I enjoy together?"

GETTING PERSONAL WITH *Linda*

♥ 1. Read Genesis 2:18–20. Why do you think God asked Adam to name all the animals right before He created his companion?

_____

_____

_____

_____ ∎

♥ 2. What are a few ways your husband would like for you to "share life with him" and "be his friend"? (You might want to ask him!)

_____

_____

_____

_____

_____

_____

_____ ∎

If a psychologist had given Jody and me personality and temperament tests before we married, he might have said, "Stop and think before you say I do!" Jody and I are not just different, we are extremely different. Jody is a thinker, I'm a feeler. He is Mr. Flow With It. I love structure. I like relational movies (he would call them soppy). He likes science fiction movies, playing chess, studying theology, and astrophysics. One year for our anniversary, I treated him to an intellectual cruise where he studied the nature and origin of the universe. He loved the academic stimulation. I loved looking out at the glorious azure blue ocean and studying in depth about intimacy with my Abba Father. As different as our interests are, we always found joy in ministering together and parenting our kids. Our kids now have kids of their own. After almost fifty years of marriage, Jody and I are still different, but we encourage each other in our "differentness" and seek to find things we enjoy together. Taking hikes in the mountains, camping in the summer, and mentoring younger couples brings intimacy and joy.

How would you like to be married to a marriage and family "expert"? Although Mike loves to tell people, "I'm sleeping with my therapist!" he's not so keen about living with someone who can "pull rank" whenever we get in an argument. If, for example, we disagree about how to discipline one of our boys, I could remind him that "I'm Doctor Juli Slattery. I think I know a little more than you do about discipline!" This is a prime example of how I could use my strength to threaten my husband instead of building him up. As I learn to use my power wisely, I see Mike appreciating my knowledge and experience as a psychologist. It is a resource for him rather than something that gives me the upper hand. But I have to choose to complete him with my strength rather than compete with him.

♥ 3. Read Proverbs 31:10–31. List the ways you see this woman being a strong companion to her husband.

_____

_____

_____

_____ ■

Companionship is lending your strength to your husband. Your strengths can be used to compete with your husband or to complete him. For example, you may have more insight into relationships than your husband does. Do you use your "woman's intuition" to help him or to keep the upper hand?

♥ 4. "The heart of her husband trusts in her . . ." (Proverbs 31:11 NASB). Part of companionship is being a trusted teammate who is willing to bring up difficult issues and even confront when necessary. However, your ability to do this is dependent upon your husband trusting you. Do you think your husband believes that you have his best interests in mind? Why or why not?

_____

_____

_____

_____ ■

Friendship takes work! Time together, communication, sacrifice, resolving conflict, communicating through difficult things. Friendship in marriage is no different. You don't become friends just because you share a house, a budget, and kids. You have to choose to build a friendship with your husband.

♥ 5. How have you used your power of companionship to build or tear down intimacy with your husband?

_____

_____

_____ ■

♥ Action Assignment: What is one thing you can do this week to work toward becoming a better friend to your husband?

_____

_____

_____

_____ ■

DAY 3
Your Power Zone: Sex

*S*am and I had been married for about ten years when I really began to ask him how he felt about sex. I knew he liked it but I just didn't get what the big deal was. So I asked him, "Do you like sex better than apple pie (his favorite dessert)?" Sam said yes. "Do you like it better than mountain biking (his favorite activity)?" Sam said yes. "If you had to choose between sex and going on vacation, what would you choose?" Sam said, "Having sex on vacation!"—Dawn

Sexuality is a powerful force. Advertisers know this—they use sex to sell everything from cars to beer. Satan knows this—he has enlisted his army of demons to distort and pervert sexuality as God intended it. Prostitutes know this—they dress provocatively and use sex to gain income. And certainly God knows this—sex is His invention and He infused within the act the ability for a man and woman to enjoy exquisite pleasure but also to create new life. But do you know this? Do you realize that your sexuality is designed to be a powerful force in your marriage? This incredible power is God-given, specifically for you as a tangible way to give and receive the deepest love and intimacy.

Let us tell you a closely kept secret about men. Men don't talk about it because they often don't know how to put this secret into words yet they know it to be true with every fiber of their being.

Closeness for him comes when you are naked body to naked body.

One husband said it like this: "After I make love with my wife, I feel whole and complete. My life is at peace."

♥ 1. Have you ever considered that your husband's sexual needs give you power in your role as a wife? Think over the years of your marriage. Write a sentence describing how you have used your power in this area of your marriage.

_____

_____

_____

_____ ∎

♥ 2. Yesterday you read Genesis 2:18–20. Read it again today through verse 25. God declares companionship as vital to a man and then He adds another need. Why do you think God mentioned both companionship and sexual intimacy in this passage?

_____

_____

_____

_____ ∎

Most women know that sex is a powerful force. The Bible is filled with examples of men who made huge mistakes because of poor sexual choices, like David and Samson. But sex is not just a negative powerful force that ruins lives. It is designed by God to be a positive powerful force for a wife in marriage. God is very specific in Scripture about describing the powerful joys and beauty of sexual love.

♥ 3. Write Proverbs 5:18–19 here:

_____

_____

_____

_____ ∎

♥ 4. How does this verse suggest that you use your sexual power as a wife?

_____

_____

_____ ▪

♥ 5. Verse 19 says that a husband is to "always be transported with delight" (AMP) in his wife's sexual love. Think about a time when you used your power wisely and transported your husband in delight through your love. What positive outcomes resulted from your choice?

_____

_____

_____

_____ ▪

♥ 6. Because sex is a power zone for a woman, it is tempting to use it to retaliate when you are angry or hurt. Reflect upon a time you foolishly abused your power by withholding the gift of sex as a means of punishing your husband. How did your actions and attitude impact "oneness" with your husband?

_____

_____

_____

_____ ▪

GETTING PERSONAL WITH *Juli*

It was many years of marriage before I realized that sex was a powerful force in my marriage. With the busyness of raising three boys, working, and managing life, I thought it was normal to let this aspect of marriage sit on the back burner. Honestly, sex just wasn't a priority for me. Then I began to see that if I didn't use my power in this area, I was allowing other women and sexual temptations to have more power in my husband's life. I became jealous of that power—it's mine! I am the one who is supposed to captivate Mike. I don't want anyone else to have the power God gave me!

The purpose of *Passion Pursuit* is to focus on what God's Word teaches about this one area of power. We want you to understand how beautiful your power is in the sexual area of marriage. We want to teach you how to allow God to reclaim and redeem your sexuality. We long to see marriages strengthened by sexual intimacy rather than destroyed by it. This is a work that God longs to do in *your* marriage!

DAY 4
Your Power Choice

The power that God has given you as a wife is like a three-legged stool. Although respect, companionship, and sexual intimacy are separate needs of a man, they also interweave and reinforce each other. When one leg of the stool is broken, the other legs are affected.

Sandy and Jim came to counseling because sexual intimacy in their marriage was dead. Sandy wanted to be intimate with her husband but he rarely seemed interested. Before marriage, Jim had talked endlessly about how much he looked forward to their sexual relationship in marriage. He couldn't keep his hands off Sandy. But now, he was completely withdrawn.

Through counseling, it became very evident that Sandy "wore the pants" in the family. She was a strong, opinionated woman who was often frustrated by her laid-back husband. Over their six years of marriage, their relationship had evolved into practically a mother-son dynamic—Sandy scolding Jim while he became more passive.

Eventually, Jim was able to communicate that the emotional climate of their relationship deeply affected his desire to be sexually intimate with Sandy. His wife's lack of confidence in him made its way to the bedroom.

Jim and Sandy's story makes it very clear that sexual intimacy doesn't occur in a vacuum. How you use your power in one area of marriage will build or tear down every aspect of intimacy.

As you dive into this study, you have a choice to make. Will you look intently at the power you have in your marriage? Will you be honest about how you have been using that power?

It's your power . . . it's your choice.

We understand that, for some of you, what you have read and heard this week has been challenging and even threatening. Based on our conversations with many women over the years, we know that your defenses might already be kicking into place. You might be thinking something like this:

"Why do I have to be the one to change? I go to all of the seminars, read all the books, but he won't lift a finger to learn to be a better husband."

"I'm afraid to even hope for intimacy in my marriage. I've been hurt and disappointed too many times."

"You just don't understand how difficult my husband is."

"If I'm honest, I'd rather be in control than learn to be intimate in my marriage. It's more important for me to feel safe than to feel close to my husband."

♥ 1. Do any of these statements represent how you are feeling as you dive into the topic of intimacy in marriage? If so, why?

_____

_____

_____ ■

♥ 2. What do you think about the message of Proverbs 14:1? Write a few sentences describing your unique power in marriage.

_____

_____

_____

_____ ■

♥ 3. Why do you think a woman would make the conscious or subconscious choice to tear down intimacy in her marriage with her power?

_____

_____

_____ ■

Not every marriage will become deeply intimate because a woman chooses to use her power to build her husband. Some relationships are riddled with serious emotional and spiritual issues that take two people to address. Although God makes no promise of resurrecting your marriage, He does make promises about the blessing that follows when a woman chooses to be faithful. The Bible is filled with assurance that the Lord sees the choices you make and that He "rewards every man (or woman) for (her) righteousness and faithfulness" (1 Samuel 26:23).

The choice about how you use your power as a wife is not just about building intimacy in marriage but about being faithful to God and trusting His promises.

No one has the power to encourage your husband like you do. More than any other human being, you are the one who knows his deepest need, his vulnerability, his areas of sensitivity, his hidden weakness. You also know better than anyone his potential as a man, his areas of talent, and his hidden strengths. You are described as a "helpmate, a counterpart, the one who comes alongside of." So ask yourself, "How do I help? How do I come alongside? How can I use the intimate knowledge of my man to build him up so that his strength may grow stronger?"

GETTING PERSONAL WITH *Linda*

I have a favorite verse that has been a key to thankfulness flowing from me to my husband. It is Philippians 4:8. I have it framed in my home because I need its wisdom continually.

Finally, whatever is true, whatever is honorable, whatever is right, whatever is pure, whatever is lovely, whatever is of good repute, if there is any excellence and if anything worthy of praise, dwell on these things. (NASB)

I took the words of Philippians 4:8 and applied them to my husband in my journal. The first few days looked like this:

Sunday—True. *Jody is committed to truth, and he lives what is true.*

Monday—Lovely (Worthy of Respect). *Jody is amazing in the way he has saved for our retirement.*

Tuesday—Just. *Jody fights for what is right and just. Whether it is evolution and creation or a political issue, he is on the side of right (or what he is convinced is right).*[4]

One choice you can make today is to choose to see your husband the way God wants you to see him. Your husband will react not only to what you do or say but how you choose to view him. It may take a step of faith for you to remember why you fell in love with this man. Underneath his weaknesses are strengths that you may have forgotten to thank God for. Finding the resolve to use your power well begins with *choosing* to be thankful for who your husband is—not complaining about who you want him to be.

4. Write Philippians 4:8 on several 3 x 5 cards and tape them where you can read this powerful verse throughout the day, or type it into your smartphone, iPad, or computer.

The verse doesn't say if **everything** is excellence *and if* **everything** *is worthy of praise*, fix your mind on these things about your husband. The word is **anything**. If you can find anything to praise your man about, dwell on that. Pretty amazing. And a key to your husband becoming a bigger and better man.

5. Meditate on Philippians 4:8. Ask God to show you praiseworthy qualities in your husband. List two or three here:

_____

_____

_____

_____

_____

_____

_____

_____ ■

♥ 6. Write a prayer to God thanking Him for your unique husband. Either show the prayer to your husband or write him an email, card, or letter expressing your thanks for who he is and what he does.

_____

_____

_____

_____

_____ ■

Bev wrote the following prayer based on Philippians 4:8:

Lord, I want to fix my eyes on everything about Gary that is true and honorable and right because Gary IS an honorable man. I want to think and act in admirable, pure, and lovely ways that make him feel safe in our relationship. I want to be a woman who is excellent and worthy of praise because he deserves no less. I want to put these things into practice—wrapped up with love and infused with a generous supply of humor, adventure, and fun. I want to keep learning and working and trying to be God's best so that God's peace will be a hedge of protection around our home, our lives, and our hearts.

When you choose to change your perspective, God changes you. Instead of seeing your husband as a workaholic, you see a disciplined man who knows how to show love through providing. Instead of an unexciting introvert, you see a man who is steady for you through the storms of life.

No matter how long you have been married, you can choose today to build intimacy in marriage with your power. Choose wisely. Speak positively. You hold power in your hands to create intimacy or distance with this man you love. And as you look to God, expect Him to do exceedingly, abundantly, more than you could ask.

DAY 5

The Secret Place: Intimacy with God

During the past four days, we challenged you to consider how to use the power you have as a wife to positively influence intimacy with your husband. We challenged you to look at how your power zones directly correspond to his basic needs for respect, companionship, and sex. We invited you to consider how you, as his wife, are uniquely qualified to fill these needs in a way no other person can. Now we're wondering: How did you respond?

Some of you are ready to dive right into the challenges. Others? Not so much.

"I want to use my power zones to make my marriage amazing but I try, I fail—I try again, I fail. Help me, God!"—Yoshiko, 28

"Respect? Companionship? Sex? I've got so far to go that I don't even know how to start."—Catherine, 37

"Power Zones? I just took power and used it like a club. Our intimacy is nonexistent."—Emily, 48

A loud chorus of wives join Yoshiko, Catherine, and Emily and say, "We can't build him up. We can't get past the disappointment and fears that intimacy represents." Throughout this study we'll ask you some difficult questions. We'll ask you to do hard things. You've already gotten a taste of this over the past few days. Perhaps you feel like the apostle Paul when he wrote:

"I have the desire to do what is good, but I cannot carry it out" (Romans 7:18).

Maybe it seems like the marriage you long for and the marriage you have today are impossibly far apart. We know this can feel like a desperate place to be. But you're not in this alone. We are beside you as friends, mentors, and fellow wives who are still learning and growing. The very best news is that your Abba Father, the One who created marriage, is also with you. His Holy Spirit's name is Encourager, Comforter, and Helper. He will give you exactly the help and encouragement you need each week—even when you have to consider questions about sex.

You've been learning about how you can use your power zones to create deeper intimacy with your husband—this is important! But the best way to move toward deeper intimacy with your husband is to move toward deeper intimacy with the Lord. You need more than power zones . . . you need the Power Source. Where is the Power found? In developing a relationship with God.

Just as in a human relationship, intimacy with God is built over time as you make the choice to know Him. Each week on Day 5, we will encourage you in another aspect of growing in intimacy with God. We are calling this special time The Secret Place. This time alone with your Abba Father equips you with the wisdom you need to respond with grace in difficulty or with love to a husband who is not acting very lovable. Jesus, God's Son, not only taught about time alone with His Father, He regularly practiced it.

🔲 I. **Read Mark 1:35 and Luke 5:16. What do you learn about Jesus and the importance of time alone with God?**

_____

_____

_____ ▪

💟 2. Read Matthew 6:6. What does this verse teach you about choosing to spend time with God?

_____

_____

_____ ■

When you choose to spend time alone with the Lord, no one will see you or reward you except your Father in heaven. Yes, it requires a sacrifice of time. You could use that time to get something done or perhaps to get an extra hour of sleep. It requires faith to believe that your time with the Lord will equip you with the power to build your marriage. Will you make it a priority?

Both of us have struggled over the years to make time alone with God a priority. Even with the best of intentions, life can get in the way and intimacy with God becomes a distant dream. We have learned, however, that we cannot do the difficult things that God asks without spending time with Him, being encouraged by His love and power. You will run into "walls" as you go through this study. Your time alone with God must be your power source if you want to change. Here are a few practical suggestions that will help you guard your time with God:

Find a place. Begin by finding a special place in your home where you can consistently be alone with God. Juli has a chair by the fireplace that is her space. Linda has a prayer chair carved in the rocks behind her home where she goes when the weather cooperates. When it doesn't, she snuggles on the couch with her Bible.

Establish a time. The next step is to carve out time to be with the Lord consistently. You might like the morning because the house is quiet. Or perhaps you are a night person. But we ask you to carve out time to study, reflect, to pray and pour out your heart to the One who loves you.

💟 3. What is the best time and place for you to regularly spend time alone with the Lord?

_____

_____

_____ ■

💟 4. What practical barriers could potentially keep you from developing an intimate friendship with God? How can you plan to prevent these barriers?

_____

_____

_____ ■

When you are alone with God this week, fall to your knees, open your hands, and pour out your heart to Him. Thank Him for what you are learning. Share your marriage joys and fears with Him. Tell Him you are desperately dependent on Him to give you the power, motivation, and strength to grow as a wife. Trust that He has designed a path for you as a wife that is uniquely yours and that He will walk beside you on each step of your journey.

5. Write a prayer to your Abba Father expressing your heart's desire for these ten weeks.

_____

_____

_____

_____

_____

_____

_____

_____

_____

_____

_____

_____

_____

_____

_____

_____

_____

_____

Me, Pursue Passion?

CHAPTER TWO

THEME:

God wants you to
pursue passion
in your marriage!

THEME VERSE:

"Eat, friends; drink
and imbibe deeply,
O lovers."
(Song of Solomon 5:1
NASB)

(From Juli) When I first met Linda, I was a clinical psychologist with sixteen years of marriage under my belt and had already written a book on sex. Even so, the Lord had much to teach me about His design for sex in marriage. I'm embarrassed to say that I had never really studied the Bible's most explicit book on sex, Song of Solomon. I didn't get it with all the jumping deer and poetry about gardens and fruit. Linda gave me the assignment to study Song of Solomon and write what I learned from the young bride about being a lover to Mike. After completing my assignment, here's what I wrote:

Every Mother's Day in recent memory, it seems that I have been confronted with the "wonder woman" of the Bible, the Proverbs 31 woman, who exemplifies a virtuous mother, wife, and community leader. I've practically memorized this section of Scripture—not because I've tried to commit it to memory but because I've read and heard the passage preached so many times.

Recently I met a new heroine in the Bible in an unlikely place. Actually, she is found in a book that for many years I just didn't understand—Song of Solomon. Like the Proverbs 31 woman, her name is not given, so I'll call her the "Smokin' Hot Mama" (SHM for short). I think SHM is even more inspiring and more convicting than Mrs. Proverbs 31! Yet, strangely, I can find no Bible studies extolling her virtues or exalting her as an example. As a young wife, no one ever pulled me aside and said, "Be like her!" Yet, my guess is that most husbands, if forced to choose, would rather have an SHM than a Proverbs 31 wife.

Perhaps churches don't put a lot of emphasis on SHM, but God's Word seems to. Look at it this way . . . the P31 woman gets half a chapter with 21 verses while SHM gets eight chapters with 117 verses. I think it's worth discovering why.

We want you to grasp a very important truth from Song of Solomon: Sexual passion —we are talking about steamy, abandoned passion between a husband and wife—is a God-honoring pursuit. Take that a step further. God actually wants you to become an exciting lover to your husband. Sexual passion in marriage isn't tainted with immorality and it isn't even a neutral, take-it-or-leave-it endeavor. It is an honorable and worthy pursuit.

Throughout this study, you'll become very familiar with Smokin' Hot Mama and Song of Solomon. We're convinced that hidden in its pages is a message that can transform intimacy in your marriage.

DAY 1

Getting to Know the Original Smokin' Hot Mama

When it comes to building intimacy, God has given us a wonderful model to study: the bride in Song of Solomon. This book contains a vivid picture of a wife who used her power to promote intimacy. The messages of this precious book are hidden, waiting to be discovered and applied by a wife like you who desperately longs for passion in her marriage.

Our God wrote the Scriptures—all sixty-six books—to teach you everything He is as Father, Son, and Spirit and to instruct you in the way of salvation and maturity. He cared so much about every area of your life—even sex—that one of the sixty-six books in the Bible is tender teaching on sexual intimacy. We think it's telling that the initials for the book Song of Solomon are SOS, the international sign for "HELP!" God knows that we need help. He knows all of the temptations we face, the fears that plague us, the wounds from the past, and the struggle of connecting sexually with a person who is so different. He has provided help through this mysterious and erotic book.

As I (Juli) confessed, I never quite understood the significance of Song of Solomon. We don't want you to minimize the powerful example of SHM because you don't quite comprehend the purpose and imagery of the book. So, the first day of homework this week is to help you understand how to read SOS.

♥ 1. Write a paragraph expressing what you think SOS is all about.

_____

_____

_____

_____ ∎

💟 2. Why do you think God chose to inspire SOS as part of His Word to us?

_____

_____

_____ ▪

The messages within SOS can seem like a mystery. At first glance, you know Solomon is writing about something sexual but you may not be sure what it all means.

Why Is the Song Difficult to Understand?

The scenes in the drama are not in chronological order.

The poetic style used in the Song is a form of Hebrew poetry called lyric idyll. One of the characteristics of this style is that the scenes are a series of flashbacks; they are not in order. If you are a logical, linear thinker (like Juli), this might be frustrating to you. However, part of the creativity expressed in the book is bringing past memories into what's happening in the moment. As you read the book, be prepared to witness erotic sex scenes and then reminisce about the wedding!

Sexual references are explained through illusive imagery and symbolism.

Recently, I (Juli) found one of my boys hiding under my desk, intently looking at my Bible. Someone in his Christian school clued him into some "interesting" Bible verses. Yes, my nine-year-old son was reading Song of Solomon! This made me *very* grateful that God inspired Solomon to use poetic imagery to portray explicit sexual acts. For example, when the husband entered his wife's "garden," the image refers to . . . well, we think you know. "Mandrakes" and "pomegranates," which spill forth their seed when opened, symbolize fertility and virility, "honey" and "wine" convey intense, erotic desire.

Perhaps God said something like this to Solomon:

Write a real-life drama that captures the passion, adventure, and mystery of marriage, but do not ignore the problems of daily life. Be frank and precise when speaking of sexual intimacy but write in such a way that if a child reads the words, his or her innocence remains intact. Regarding sexual activity, be specific enough to be helpful, but sensitive enough not to offend. Be spiritual, yet practical; wholesome, yet sensuous. And do it all in one hundred and twenty verses or less!¹

The end result is a book on sex that is specific, yet poetic. Frank, yet innocent. Simple, yet profound. Confusing, yet straightforward. Truly, the Song is an amazing little book. We are excited and expectant as we lead you into the riches of Song of Solomon because it is here you discover all that it means to be a Smokin' Hot Mama!

What Is the Song About?

The first part of the Song addresses the passions and insecurities faced by most newlyweds. We witness the king and his lovely virgin bride as they run to the bedroom to consummate their marriage. Heat rises from the pages as we view the steamy, yet appropriate, exchange of endearments and caresses. Then, toward the middle of the Song, problems surface. Selfishness rears its ugly head as SHM dreams about a recurring problem in their sexual relationship. In the dream, Solomon comes to SHM late at night, demanding sex. She rejects him because she wants to sleep, then she feels bad, and runs after him. Near the end, the book expresses one of the most powerful statements in the Bible about married love: "True love is stronger than death, it is eternal and everlasting, the very flame of the Lord" (Song 8:6, our paraphrase of NASB).

Literal or Figurative?

There is much debate about whether the Song should be interpreted literally (about sexual intimacy in marriage) or figuratively (about God's relationship with His people). As you will learn next week, sexual intimacy is a metaphor God uses to describe intimacy with His chosen people. We believe that the Song is both literal and figurative. However, throughout this study, we will be studying it as it relates to marital intimacy.

Why Should You Listen to Solomon?

Solomon doesn't seem like the perfect lover model—he had hundreds of wives. First, let us say we've asked the "Why Solomon?" questions, too. It is important to know that Solomon inherited many of his wives and concubines from his father; others he acquired for political alliances. Also, 1 Kings indicates it wasn't until later in his life that Solomon accumulated all his wives, which were his downfall (1 Kings 11:4). Even so, we still think Solomon lacks the proper credentials for giving anyone—let alone Christians—marital advice. We just weren't sure we could trust Solomon. But we do trust God! Solomon's resume has one positive credential that overshadows all his weaknesses as a writer for a book about married love. God chose Solomon to write the Song.[2]

💟 3. It's time to open your Bible and read Song of Solomon from beginning to end. It is only eight chapters and shouldn't take you long. Write down any new observations you have now that you better understand how the book was written.

_____

_____

_____ ■

💟 4. How would you describe the "main characters" in SOS?

_____

_____

_____ ■

♥ 5. What do you think the Lord wants to teach you through studying Song of Solomon and SHM?

_____

_____

_____ ∎

♥ 6. Write a prayer to the Lord expressing your thoughts to Him for including SOS in the Bible. Tell Him what you desire to learn through studying this book over the next few days.

_____

_____

_____

_____

_____

_____ ∎

DAY 2

SHM: A Woman Who Knew How to Use Her Power

Do you remember the theme verse from last week, Proverbs 14:1? If not, here's a refresher: "The wise woman builds her house, but with her own hands the foolish one tears hers down." You studied how to use your power wisely as a wife.

While the verse says that you build or tear down intimacy with your "hands," we've learned that the mouth seems to be more involved than hands. Perhaps we could rephrase the verse like this: "The wise woman builds her house, but with her own *mouth* the foolish one tears hers down."

All we know about SHM and her smokin' hot relationship is captured in the words of Song of Solomon. By her words, we can tell that she made the choice to use her power wisely. Today we want to study how the Smokin' Hot Mama skillfully used her three areas of power to build smokin' hot intimacy in her marriage. She praised her husband, became his intimate friend, and delighted in sexual love with him.

♥ 1. Read Song of Solomon 2:3–13 and 5:10–16. List all of the ways the SHM describes her husband.

_____

_____

_____ ■

♥ 2. Based on her description, what picture do you have in your mind of Solomon?

_____

_____

_____ ■

♥ 3. How did the SHM use her words to build confidence in her husband?

_____

_____

_____ ■

♥ 4. Read Song of Solomon 7:9–8:3. What do you think is happening here? How does SHM use her words to entice her husband sexually?

_____

_____

_____ ■

♥ 5. How do you think this wife is using her power of respect, friendship, and sexuality in these verses?

_____

_____

_____ ■

We see the idea of companionship and sexual intimacy linked together beautifully in Song of Solomon 5:16. We think this is one of the most powerful verses about marriage in

Scripture. Because this verse can be a game changer in your intimacy, we are going to ask you to memorize it—and to take it a step further and go "beyond memorization." What do we mean by that? We want you to go beyond knowing the words, to press the words into your spirit in such a way that it infiltrates your very being and causes new thoughts and actions to spring forth.

♥ 6a. WRITE Song of Solomon 5:16 here:

_____

_____

_____

_____ ■

6b. MEMORIZE it—repeat it over and over until the words flow easily from your lips.

6c. MEDITATE on the beauty of the message. What does it mean that your husband is your lover and your friend? How do you express the reality of these two ideas in your marriage?

_____

_____

_____ ■

6d. PERSONALIZE the verse by writing a prayer to God. Carol's prayer looked like this:

Wow, God, this is one passionate wife. Her husband is altogether desirable to her. She loves his kisses. And what I think is most beautiful is that her husband is not only her lover, he is her friend. God, I want this to be real for my man and me. Please let me see him as wholly desirable, as friend, lover, partner in life. Oh I want this to be true for us!

Wow! _____

_____

_____

_____

_____

_____ ■

DAY 3

A Woman Who Had Permission

From Juli:

The first time I really studied Smokin' Hot Mama, I was amazed to see how this young wife pursued passion. She had insecurities about her body and her ability to please her husband, just like I do. Yet she was so free with her body, her mind, and her words. Here are a few observations I had about SHM.

Proactive

SHM is not a wife who waits around for her man to bring up the idea of sex. She proactively thinks about her husband, anticipates sex, and entices him. In Christian circles, I've often heard that the "good Christian wife" responds to her husband's advances. But SHM is way beyond that—she is sexually proactive. She aggressively pursues, captivates, and loves her husband.

Uninhibited

SHM's thoughts, words, and actions can almost be described as "over the top." It seems as if she just can't find a way to adequately express how in love she is and how completely she hopes to be satisfied in sexual love. Nothing holds her back.

Honest

She is honest that she feels insecure about how she looks compared with other women. Most women can identify with SHM's insecurities about her appearance but she doesn't stay there. When her husband responds with praise and the reassurance that he delights in her, she doesn't argue or resist. Instead, she embraces his praise, and by the end of the book we find her standing assuredly in the admiring gaze of her husband as a confident lover who knows that she can satisfy him.

Powerful

She is a wife who knows how to use her sexual power. She employs the full scope of her sexuality—words, actions, thoughts, and planning—to capture her husband's love. When they have a quarrel she responds by pursuing him with praise and sexual enticement rather than punishing him by withholding what she knows will recapture his heart.

Discreet

Although SHM is a bold, confident lover, she is not considered a brazen woman that men are warned to avoid, like the one described in Proverbs 5:1–6. Why? She is passionate, vocal, and unrestrained, but exclusively within the confines of married love. All of her fantasies are about her husband and their intimate oneness. She understands that her sexuality was designed to be fully expressed—body, soul, and spirit—to arouse and satisfy *only* her husband.

Do you wonder how this young wife became the Smokin' Hot Mama? What in her past made her free to be such a wonderful, abandoned lover to her husband? How did she get to be so unrestrained? We believe that an event recorded in Song of Solomon is a key to understanding her passion pursuit. We shared about this scene in the message this week. Now we want you to take a look at it.

♥ 1. Read Song 4:16–5:1 and write a paragraph describing what's happening here.

_____

_____

_____

_____

_____

_____ ▪

The wedding night scene in Song of Solomon 4:1–16 and 5:1 is holy and erotic. Did we just use those two words together—in a Bible study? We did. As Solomon and his bride lay wrapped in each other's arms in the afterglow of their sexual love, another presence enters the room, and the scene is momentarily suspended because an announcement is about to be made.

Seriously? Someone invades the privacy of these lovers? Someone intrudes upon this steamy yet holy scene to make an announcement? Yes! The Holy One, the God of Israel. We know, some Bible commentators attribute these words as being spoken by the "daughters of Jerusalem." We disagree. We agree with the position taken by Dr. Charles Ryrie and Dr. Tremper Longman who say this is indeed the voice of God because a blessing of this stature must come from a higher authority.[3] Who could encourage the king and queen to fully partake in the pleasure of erotic love? None other than the Lord Almighty, the King of the universe—and the Author and Creator of sexual love.

It is as if God walked over to the bridal bed, put out His hand in blessing, and spoke this benediction over the couple: "Eat, friends; drink and imbibe deeply, O lovers" (5:1 NASB).

If we told you the original Hebrew translation of these words, the potency of God's blessing would steal your breath away as He encourages the lovers to imbibe in sexual intoxication. Imagine! Our Holy God says, "Be intoxicated with your sexual love! Your sexual union is right, pure, and beautiful."

The Creator God approves and endorses your abandonment in giving yourselves freely to each other as husband and wife. How amazing, how holy and overwhelming, that your Father God cares so much about your sexual intimacy that He made sure a "Blessing Ceremony" was hidden in His Word.

GETTING PERSONAL WITH *Linda*

I grew up with a wonderful mother and an abusive alcoholic father. What I saw of intimacy between my parents was my drunken father dragging my mother into the bedroom. I hated what I thought he would do to her. A psychologist (right, Dr. Juli?) would have said I could have trouble enjoying sex in marriage. But at age twenty I embraced Christ as my Savior, and God's Word became my guidebook for all of life, including sexuality. I saw in Scripture (especially in Song of Solomon) a free, glorious intimacy and, because it was in God's Word, I believed it and gave myself permission for passion. My Abba Father was so gracious to give Jody and me the gift of delightful passion from the beginning of our marriage. Yes, He is a good God to take a young woman who had negative thoughts in her mind about sex, who had made some wrong choices, and bless her with sexual freedom and joy. I remember in the early years of our marriage asking Jody to share with me his picture of his dream lover, which he was happy to share, and then me saying, "This is who I want to become!"

2. Why do you think God chose to include this "Blessing Ceremony" in His Holy Word? What implications does this have for how a Christian couple should think about their sexual relationship?

_____

_____

_____

_____

_____

_____

3. How do you think having God's blessing on sexual intimacy influenced SHM's approach to sex in her marriage?

_____

_____

_____

_____

_____

Does God really care that much about sex that He would inspire Solomon to write a sex manual for married couples to learn from? The message that God cares about intimacy in your marriage is not limited to SOS.

4. Look up Deuteronomy 24:5 and write it here:

_____

_____

_____

_____

_____

_____

_____

_____ ■

Of all the books in the Bible, you probably didn't expect to find a reference to the importance of sex in Deuteronomy! The Hebrew word *samach*, translated here as "bring happiness," carries the idea of "to gladden, make someone merry." Dr. Howard Hendricks says that this "expression encompasses happiness in all areas but certainly includes sexual delight."[4]

Most of us didn't apply this verse during our first year of marriage. Whether you've been married one year, nineteen years like Juli, or almost fifty like Linda, this can be your special season to spend time learning, concentrating, and praying about how to bring sexual happiness to your husband and him to you. It is a worthy goal and one that pleases your God.

Solomon and his bride were naked and unashamed when their Creator God appeared in their bedroom, walked over to their bridal bed, and blessed them. God's blessing gives you permission to be abandoned in exploring each other's bodies and expressing love. Will you give *yourself* permission?

DAY 4

Where's My Permission Slip?

Does it seem strange to you that God would want you to become a passionate wife? Do you really believe He wants you to become like Smokin' Hot Mama? If it seems a little "out there" for you, you are not alone. Many wives struggle with the idea that pursuing passion is something that pleases God.

"Me, passionate? I think I must have been absent the day God was passing out passion."

"How can you be passionate when you are a hundred pounds overweight?"

"I've tried to be passionate with my husband, but he didn't respond. I don't think I want to set myself up for that rejection again."

"We have so much junk in our marriage. The things we've done, what we've said . . . it all just feels dirty and way beyond God's blessing."

You might be able to get your mind around the idea that God blesses the seemingly "perfect" union represented in Song of Solomon. But what about your own very imperfect marriage? Does God "bless" the sexual union between a husband and wife who have brought pain and baggage into the bedroom?

The answer is YES.

We know you may face some significant barriers to accepting God's blessing on sexual intimacy in your marriage. But we want you to hear this loud and clear: God has blessed the sexual relationship between you and your husband. No matter what you've done, how much you've struggled, what baggage you brought into marriage, or how warped sex has become between you, God desires to redeem and restore the passion between you and your husband. His blessing and His permission are for you!

One very smart husband understood this and when his wife, Heidi, asked what he wanted for his birthday, his unusual response left her speechless. "Heidi, all I want for my birthday is for you to give yourself permission to enjoy, really enjoy, passionate sex."

Perhaps the most powerful message in Song of Solomon is that God is calling married couples to pursue sexual passion. In fact, becoming a Smokin' Hot Mama involves partnering with God to reclaim the beautiful gift that sin has distorted. It is holy and right for a married woman to move toward passionate intimacy. We can't say it enough: *God wants to bless your sexual relationship with your husband.*

When God first created a man and woman in the garden of Eden, sexual oneness was an important aspect of their relationship.

1. Read Genesis 2:21–24 and paraphrase what happened in these verses.

_____

_____

_____

_____

2. Write Genesis 2:25.

_____

_____

_____

3. What is the significance of this verse?

_____

_____

_____

♥ 4. Read Genesis 3:7. What happened after Adam and Eve sinned? What impact did this have on their sexual intimacy?

_____

_____

_____ ■

As a result of sin, nakedness and sexuality are often linked with shame. Your sexual relationship, even with your husband, may have a history of shame and sin that make it difficult to accept that God blesses your sexual union. The great news is that by dying on the cross, Jesus Christ took your shame upon Him. In every aspect of your life, including sexual intimacy, He invites you to pursue what is right and good without shame.

♥ 5. What aspects of sexual intimacy in marriage do you feel that you don't have permission to pursue? How does feeling shame keep you from accepting God's blessing?

_____

_____

_____ ■

♥ 6. How would it change your approach to sexual intimacy if you agreed that God wanted you to be a passionate lover in marriage?

_____

_____

_____ ■

♥ 7. Write a statement of permission from God to you and your husband.

_____

_____

_____ ■

One woman's permission statement:

You, My daughter, have My complete blessing to unwrap every gift of love I have given to you and Alan. Feast on your lovemaking—enjoy each touch, each sigh, each sensation. Delight in the secrets that only you share. Drink deeply of the love I have given you. Guard it and protect it, for it is sacred.

DAY 5

The Secret Place: Take a Step!

I wish God would write me a personal letter or email telling me what He thinks about me and my marriage. I've heard people say that the Bible is "God's love letter" to me, but how do I know that the words apply to me personally? How can I believe that the message of Song of Solomon applies to me? Can I really believe that God wants me to be a Smokin' Hot Mama?—Graciela

The answer to Graciela's question? *TAKE A STEP OF FAITH.*

This study will teach your brain some new concepts about marriage and sexuality. It might challenge your ways of thinking. But in order for it to change your marriage, you have to be willing to take a step of faith. You hold a permission slip in your hands, telling you and your husband to go after a passionate sex life. You have to believe, by faith, that this message written thousands of years ago is also God's inspired Word for you.

The eleventh chapter of Hebrews is often called "The Faith Hall of Fame." It records a number of men and women who made choices based on their great faith in God.

💟 1. Write Hebrews 11:1 here.

_____

_____

_____

_____ ▪

💟 2. According to this verse, what does it mean to have faith?

_____

_____

_____

_____

_____ ▪

The Bible calls Abraham the "Father of our faith." His story is recorded in the book of Genesis. Several authors of the New Testament also teach about the faith he demonstrated.

♥ 3. Read Romans 4:20–21. What does this passage say about Abraham's example of faith?

_____

_____

_____ ■

This passage says that Abraham was "fully persuaded that God had power to do what he had promised." Faith requires that we put our confidence and belief in what God has said. It goes beyond what we think; it impacts the way we behave.

Claire Took a Step of Faith

If ever a wife was hung up about sex, it was Claire—and for good reason. Given into child pornography by her mother, Claire learned about sex in hideous, horrible ways. She determined never to marry. The problem was that her best friend was a guy and he wanted to marry her. After he proposed several times, Claire finally said yes and thought, *Okay, I'll just have to deal with the sex stuff.* But she couldn't deal with it. Every time they made love, Claire had a panic attack.

After three children and several years of marriage, Claire read a book coauthored by Linda called *Intimate Issues* about God's perspective on sex and thought, "This can't be true. It can't!" Then she read Song of Solomon and said, "I see it in God's Word and, if it is in God's Word, I'll believe it."

Claire didn't stop there. It wasn't enough just to have her thinking changed. She chose to act on the new truth God had given her. In spite of her fear, Claire bravely took a step of faith by re-creating her wedding night and inviting her husband to begin their intimate oneness all over again.

Was this step easy for Claire? Absolutely not. She had to fight through the pain of past memories, fear of vulnerability, and her feelings of shame. But Claire told me (Linda) that it was the beginning of a new joy in their sexual intimacy that flowed over to all areas of their marriage.

Taking a step of faith is difficult but we know you want to pursue passion. So, friend, grab your Nikes and get ready to step!

Your step of faith will be unique to the challenges you face in the pursuit of passion. Perhaps you are not ready for a "leap" like Claire's. God might be asking you to take a small, yet brave step, like Lauren:

While in prayer, I resolved to break a vow I'd made many years before to not initiate sex. Though my whispered and veiled attempt at initiating sex was so meager he did not even have a clue as to what I was offering (much like offering someone a little white marshmallow on a stick with no nearby fire to roast it). At least I took a tiny step in the right direction. Maybe next time, I'll have the courage and ability to build the fire too.

What kind of step is God asking you to take toward pursuing passion? Here are a couple of suggestions:

- Write your husband a letter telling him that you want to work on pursuing passion in your marriage.
- Initiate a sexual encounter with your husband this week.
- Memorize verses from Song of Solomon that remind you of the permission God gives you to pursue passion.
- Call a friend or counselor to begin to bring light to shame that has been hidden for many years.

4. Write a prayer to the Lord asking Him to give you the strength to take a step of faith that is unique to you.

_____

_____

_____

_____

_____

_____

_____

_____

_____

_____

_____

_____

let's pray

_____

_____

_____

_____

_____

God's Got an Opinion!

Everyone's got an opinion about sex—your mother, your hairdresser, your friends, and we're sure your husband does too. But did you know that God also has an opinion . . . a definite, distinct perspective? Does that surprise you?

Where is God's opinion about sex expressed? You might think that the church and its leaders would be the place to discover God's opinion about sex—after all, these are the ones who claim to speak for Him. But as we search the records of history, our hearts are distressed because often the church and her leaders have adopted attitudes that express their own opinions rather than God's opinion.

In AD 200 this was how the church viewed sex:

Church authorities issued edicts forbidding sex on Thursdays, the day of Christ's arrest; on Fridays, the day of his death; on Saturdays, in honor of the Blessed Virgin; and on Sundays in honor of the departed saints. Wednesdays sometimes made the list too, as did the 40-day fast periods before Easter, Christmas, and Pentecost, and also feast days and days of the Apostles, as well as the days of female impurity. The list escalated until only 44 days a year remained available for marital sex![1]

Does this surprise you? If so, you'll be even more surprised to learn that some of the church's most godly men viewed passion in sex as a sin:

Nothing is so much to be shunned as sex relations.—St. Augustine

Intercourse is never without sin; but God excuses it by his grace because the estate of marriage is his work.—Martin Luther

If these statements leave you flabbergasted, consider this statement from Peter Lombard, a respected theologian who lived in the twelfth century:

The Holy Spirit leaves the room when a married couple has sex, even if they do it without passion.

 We wonder, where did the Holy Spirit go? Did He hide under the kitchen table or in a closet? You may think it was just the godly men who were a bit misguided but listen to this information given to young brides in the late 1800s from a godly pastor's wife:

To the sensitive young woman who has had the benefits of proper upbringing, the wedding day is, ironically, both the happiest and most terrifying day of her life. On the positive side, there is the wedding itself, on the negative side, there is the wedding night, during which the bride must "pay the piper," so to speak, by facing for the first time the terrible experience of sex.

At this point, let me concede one shocking truth. Some young women actually anticipate the wedding night ordeal with curiosity and pleasure! Beware such an attitude! One cardinal rule of marriage should never be forgotten: GIVE LITTLE, GIVE SELDOM, AND ABOVE ALL, GIVE GRUDGINGLY.[2]

Really? How do you suppose her husband felt about such advice? Even more importantly, how does God feel about the advice offered through the centuries by those claiming to represent Him? We feel certain that the motivation behind the statements of these godly men and women was not to put a moratorium on sex but rather to reinforce the idea of holy days and holy practices that would honor God. But the underlying message contained a destructive lie: holiness and sex are incompatible bed partners.

Fortunately in recent years Christian leaders have espoused attitudes that contain a very different message.

If anyone says that sex in itself is bad, Christianity contradicts him at once.—C. S. Lewis[3]

While sex is not the only aspect of physical relationship in a marriage, it is in most cases the most important one, the touchstone for everything else from smiles and daily gestures of tenderness to deeds of kindness and sacrifice . . . the whole challenge of marital life is simply to catch up in all other departments with the pure rapture of the physical relationship at its best.—Mike Mason[4]

A married couple gives a severe blow to the head of that ancient serpent when they aim to give as much sexual satisfaction to each other as possible. Is it not a mark of amazing grace that on top of all the pleasure that the sexual side of marriage brings, it also proves to be a fearsome weapon against our ancient foe? . . .

Marriage at its exquisite peak of pleasure speaks powerfully the truth of covenant-keeping love between Christ and his church. And that love is the most powerful force in the world.—John Piper[5]

No wonder Christian couples are confused! Who speaks for God—the religious leaders and institutions that imply that sexual passion is a sin or those who say sexual intimacy between a husband and wife is blessed and holy?

It comes down to this: if we listen to the opinions of man (and woman), we will be confused. If we truly want to know God's opinion about sex, then we must listen to God Himself. Where do we find God's true opinion? Only in His Word. So open your Bible. Open wide your heart. Fling open your spiritual eyes and uncover your spiritual ears because what we will discuss during these next five days has the potential to turn your thinking upside down.

God's teaching on sex begins in the first few pages of the Bible. In Genesis we read that God created sexual intimacy for Adam and Eve. You already know that one of the reasons God gave the gift of sex was so that Adam and Eve could fulfill God's command "to multiply," so we won't spend time talking about "birthing babies." Instead we'll focus on the less obvious reasons why He gave the gift of sex and how these reasons reveal His opinions about sex. This week we want to explore three intimacy gifts hidden in the pages of Scripture that the Lord longs for you to open:

1. The Gift of Intimate Knowing
2. The Gift of Holy Intimacy
3. The Gift of Exquisite Pleasure

Each of these gifts will encourage you to grow in deeper intimacy with your husband. Each of these gifts will reveal God's clear and distinct opinions about sex. So get ready because you are in for fun and maybe a surprise or two!

DAY 1

Where Did You Get Your Opinion about Sex?

What has formed your sexual perspective? Your sexual mindset has been affected by the positive and negative messages passed down through the centuries. All you have seen and heard during your growing up years—every right choice about your sexuality and every wrong choice. Any evil done to you has deeply impacted you.

As we have the privilege to travel around the world speaking to wives about sex, we see confusion—mass confusion—among God's women. They look at the world's distortion of sex: the exploitation of the female body and the vulgarity of how sex is portrayed. Some women respond to this by thinking, "I don't want to have anything to do with sex. It's just disgusting!" Yet this attitude is just as wrong as the world's.

Where did we get our sexual mindsets? Where did you get yours? And what is a mindset anyway? "A mindset is a collection of individual thoughts that over a period of time influence the way we perceive life."[6]

Today is a day for you to reflect with your God. Find a half hour alone (this is hard but possible) and ask God to give you His wisdom in answering the following questions.

As you begin your special time alone with God, will you pray?

God, I know I have some wrong thoughts in my mind about sex. Today I'm asking You for answers. Will You please help me see where these wrong thoughts came from and show me how to unravel the mixed-up sexual thoughts in my mind? I know I need to understand this to get to Your opinion about sex.

♥ 1. What did you learn about sexual intimacy in your home?

_____

_____

_____ ▪

♥ 2. What did you learn from friends, movies, and TV?

_____

_____

_____ ▪

♥ 3. How did messages from the church influence you in a positive or negative way?

_____

_____

_____ ▪

♥ 4. How did the things you learned influence you when you married?

_____

_____

_____ ▪

♥ 5. Write a paragraph describing your sexual mindset today.

_____

_____

_____ ■

♥ 6. Write a prayer to God expressing how you desire Him to change your opinion about sex to match His opinion.

_____

_____

_____

_____ ■

DAY 2

Open the Gift of Intimate Knowing

The first aspect to the gift God has given you and your husband in your sexuality is the ability to know, really know, each other intimately. Women often see sex as a way to express the deep love and appreciation they have for their husbands. However, we hope you also see that it is a way to build deep love and appreciation. Yes, emotional intimacy prepares you for sex. But sex also prepares you for emotional intimacy.

In this week's message we looked at two often overlooked facts that prove that sex is for the purpose of deep and intimate bonding: the biology of brain chemistry and the theology of intimate knowing.

Oxytocin: The Biology of Brain Chemistry

God's creation is beyond amazing! Did you know that God created your body to release chemicals in your brain that deeply bond you to your husband and him to you? That bonding is reinforced through sexual expression. The power of hormones like oxytocin help you and your husband to "feel" in love, to focus on each other's strengths, and even to weather conflict in marriage. The hormones released during sex actually train your brain to love your husband and for him to love you!

Yada: The Theology of Intimate Knowing

The Hebrew word used in the Old Testament for "to know deeply" is *yada*. It is an active form of knowing, pursuing, and experiencing. *Yada* is used to indicate a knowing of facts, the learning of skill, and even of the deep knowing in sexual intercourse. In Genesis 4:1 we read, "And Adam knew (yada) Eve as his wife, and she became pregnant and bore Cain" (AMP).

When you and your husband are together sexually, it's about more than biology, more than exchanging body fluids and releasing chemicals in the brain. God desires you to deeply know each other physically, emotionally, and spiritually. Anything less is a compromise, an inadequate expression of what God designed. Through God's gift of Intimate Knowing, a husband and wife receive a deep knowledge of each other that they have with no one else. This knowing brings a depth to their relationship. Who could have imagined all of that could be accomplished by sex? As we said in week 1, sex is very, very powerful.

Mike Mason expresses it beautifully in *The Mystery of Marriage*.

For in touching a person of the opposite sex in the most secret place of his or her body, with one's own most private part, there is something that reaches beyond touch, that gets behind flesh itself to the place where it connects with spirit, to the place where incarnation happens.[7]

This quote takes the Gift of Intimate Knowing to a lofty level and is beautiful. A young wife makes it practical, which is also beautiful:

"I had no idea sex would be like this. It's as if we have a secret sexual language. Jake looks at me in my jeans and sweater but his smile says, "I see you without them—I know every curve, I know what turns you on. Your body is mine—all mine—only mine!" Or my smile can say across a room filled with people, "Ten more minutes and let's get out of here and have our own private party." —Debbie

Sometimes when the Bible references sex within marriage, it does so with words like holiness or honor, which are wonderful but a bit vague. If you are like us, you want more specifics of how this looks. There's no better place to discover this in the poetic yet specific details in Song of Solomon.

Let's learn some secrets about *yada* from Smokin' Hot Mama.

1. Read Song of Solomon 4:1–16. List the ways the SHM "knows" or "pursues" her husband.

_____

_____

_____

_____

♥ 2. *Yada* is about more than knowing your husband. It is also about being willing to be known. Now list all of the ways you see SHM allowing herself to be known in Song of Solomon, chapter 4.

_____

_____

_____ ■

♥ 3. What excites you about *yada* sex with your husband?

_____

_____

_____ ■

♥ 4. Does anything about *yada* sex with your husband cause a trickle of fear in your heart?

_____

_____

_____ ■

Maybe you had a tough time answering question 3 because you think, *Our sexual relationship is a far cry from yada—it's more like nada* (the Spanish word for "nothing"). If sexual intimacy with your husband is practically nonexistent or so dull and predictable that you want to fall asleep in the middle of making love, it's likely you have some obstacles in the way. We will address some of these obstacles in the weeks to come. However, even through the process of addressing problems in your sexual relationship, God will help you know and discover each other. Some of the most intimate marriages have been forged through the determination to know each other through forgiveness, mercy, and healing.

> *"Both my husband and I were wounded in our sexuality so it seemed impossible for us to experience yada. How could we know each other deeply when we'd both put up walls to keep out the pain? As I look back, I see that it was through the pain, in the process of being healed individually and together, that this knowing of one another began. I thank God for the problems and hurts . . . they have taken us deeper."*—Janae

♥ 5. How has your sexual relationship enabled you to know your husband physically, sexually, and emotionally in ways that otherwise would not have been possible?

_____

_____

_____ ■

♥ 6. List one way you can seek to know your husband more completely through sex this week and one way you can allow yourself to be more completely known. Then plan an intimate encounter in the coming weeks in which you intentionally practice these concepts.

_____

_____

_____ ■

What is God's opinion about sex? The first gift we unwrapped, The Gift of Intimate Knowing, whispers: "There is a secret knowing in sex that is precious beyond words."

DAY 3

Open the Gift of Holy Intimacy

"The ultimate reason (not the only reason) why we are sexual is to make God more deeply knowable." —John Piper[8]

Take a moment to meditate on this statement from John Piper. What do you think he means? How could the primary purpose of sex be to make God more deeply knowable? Piper didn't just come up with this idea on his own—it's a reflection of what the Bible teaches about sex. The images of marriage and of sexuality are woven throughout Scripture. The Old Testament frequently refers to Israel as God's bride. The New Testament describes the church (the body of believers) as Christ's bride. In the book of Ephesians, the apostle Paul interweaves the relationship of husband and wife with the relationship of Christ and the church.

♥ 1. Write Ephesians 5:31–32 here.

_____

_____

_____ ■

♥ 2. Paul says that the "one flesh" sexual union of a husband and wife is a picture of Christ and His bride, the church. Why is it hard for us to get our minds around this picture?

_____

_____

_____ ∎

We both struggled to make sense of this verse.

(*Linda*:) I pondered Ephesians 5:31–32 for many years. I knew God was trying to show me something about the degree of closeness He wanted me to have spiritually with Christ, but I couldn't quite get it because sex is so physical: the sights, the sounds, and even the mess.

(*Juli:*) It's only been within the last year that I've begun to understand some part of the "mystery" of sex signifying unity with Christ. It dawned on me that everything God has created reveals something about Him. Why should the act of sex be any different— particularly when He specifically says in His Word what it is meant to symbolize?

We confess, we are still grasping to understand this mystery. As we press deeper into what Paul is saying, we see surprising truths: Sex is not only meant to bond you to your husband, it's a mysterious reflection of the union the Holy God desires to have with us. The passion, the longing for unity, and the expression of love through sex are meant to reflect a spiritual reality of God's desire for us and ours for Him. His desire is for nothing short of complete oneness.

As Paul says, this is a mystery. Although we cannot fully understand it in our humanity, the mystery clearly points to the fact that sex, as God designed it, is very spiritual and very holy.

Clifford and Joyce Penner in their book *The Gift of Sex* amplify the mystery:

> Ephesians 5:31–32 is basically saying that the sexual relationship is what best symbolizes the relationship between Christ and the church. We have to assume that this symbolism is telling us that there is something more to sex

GETTING PERSONAL WITH *Linda*

I wonder what you are thinking as you read about holy intimacy and the mystery of sexual union. If you think my theologian husband, Jody, and I talk about this mystery and always feel "holy" when making love, think again. I remember sharing Mike Mason's quote (p. 48) with Jody and he looked at me as I read about "flesh connecting with spirit" and said, "I just know it feels *great* and that's what's important to me."

than physical release, since our sexual relationship is a model of how we can best understand God's desire to have an intense relationship with us.

Furthermore, it seems clear that if God, in communicating through the Scripture, chooses to use sexual terms to describe his relationship with us, then we may assume that this is a hearty endorsement of the sexual part of ourselves.[9]

Yesterday you discovered that when the Hebrew word *yada* is used in the Bible in reference to sexual intimacy in marriage, it refers to a deep and active pursuit to know and be known. The word *yada* is also used to reflect the way God wants us to know Him. As we said, Genesis 4:1 uses *yada* sexually: "And Adam knew Eve his wife and she bore a son." Jeremiah 16:21 uses *yada* to know God spiritually: "Therefore behold, I am going to make them know (*yada*)—This time I will make them know (*yada*) My power and My might; and they shall know (*yada*) that My name is the Lord" (NASB).

Are you beginning to glimpse the height, depth and breadth of *yada*?

♥ 3. Write Psalm 46:10 here.

_____

_____

_____ ∎

Guess what Hebrew word is translated into "know" here? You guessed it . . . *yada*. Regardless of what you have been taught in church or what was modeled for you by your parents, God is not a distant Father. He longs to know His children and for them to know Him intimately.

♥ 4. Write a letter to a young bride explaining the beauty of these verses (Ephesians 5:31–32 and Psalm 46:10). Share with her why the gift of holy intimacy is so special.

_____

_____

_____

_____

HOLY _____

_____

_____ ∎

♥ 5. How does understanding that God sees sex as holy change how you view intimacy with your husband?

_____

_____

_____ ■

This is the opinion of the Lord God Almighty, Creator of heaven and earth:
Sexual passion in marriage is not only beautiful; it is very, very holy.

♥ 6. Write a prayer asking your Father God to make the holiness of the gift of intimate oneness real in your mind and heart and actions.

_____

_____

_____

_____ ■

DAY 4
Open the Gift of Exquisite Pleasure

O*ur God, who is spirit, can be found behind the very physical panting, sweating, and pleasurable entangling of limbs and body parts. He doesn't turn away. He wants us to run into sex but to do so with his presence, priorities, and virtues marking our pursuit.*"—Gary Thomas[10]

We told you God has an opinion about sex. He also has an opinion about pleasure. He is wholeheartedly, enthusiastically, unequivocally in favor of out-of-this-world sexual pleasure in marriage. How do we know? Pleasure was God's idea. He thought it up. He could have created sex with no pleasure—just push a button on each other's bodies at the appropriate time and Voila! a baby is conceived. No pleasure. No ecstatic delight. Definitely not God's plan.

We wonder, what was God thinking when He created the bodies of the man and woman to fit together perfectly in order to send them into rapture? Perhaps He thought something like this:

Intimate Knowing is good. Holy Intimacy is very good. My blessing is very, very good. But I will do something even more with this gift—I will enable My man and woman to give and receive intoxicating pleasure, an explosion of ecstasy that will create a deep longing for them to come together often.

Yes, God puts His stamp of approval on sexual pleasure but only in the confines of a marriage between one husband and one wife. Does God have an opinion about sexual pleasure outside the boundaries of marriage? Absolutely. Let's look at an example in Proverbs 5 where God first strongly denounces sexual pleasure expressed outside the marriage bed and then strongly urges sexual pleasure within marriage.

♥ 1. Read Proverbs 5:1–19.

a. Summarize verses 1–14.

_____

_____

_____ ▪

b. An abrupt change occurs in verses 15–19. Paraphrase these verses here:

_____

_____

_____ ▪

c. Describe what the images of "water," "cisterns," and "running water from your own well" depict in Proverbs 5:15.

_____

_____

_____ ▪

> May your fountain be blessed, and may you rejoice in the wife of your youth. A loving doe, a graceful deer—may her breasts satisfy you always, may you ever be captivated by her love. (Proverbs 5:18–19)

♥ 2. Write a contemporary, beautiful, yet erotic, version of these verses.

_____

_____

_____ ▪

Are you surprised that God's Word (His holy Word) talks about a husband delighting in his wife's breasts? This surprises us.

Linda shares a literal translation of Proverbs 5:19:

Let your love and your sexual embrace with your wife, intoxicate you continually with delight. Always enjoy the ecstasy of her love.

♥ 3. Write a paragraph describing how a husband would feel if his wife's goal was to intoxicate him with sexual delight.

_____

_____

_____

_____ ■

Proverbs 5 is addressed to a man but the pleasure described goes both ways. The husband is intoxicated by the sexual love of his wife and she is overtaken by the sexual pleasure she receives.

LOVE

We have met many women who read these verses but can't quite accept that God delights in a married couple enjoying exquisite sexual love. Are you one of them? Perhaps you learned about sexual pleasure through the tainted lens of premarital sex, pornography, or sexual abuse. The fact that Satan has twisted God's beautiful design does not forfeit God's plan of sexual pleasure for your marriage!

♥ 4. Do you know what brings your husband pleasure in intimacy? Does he know what brings you pleasure? Set aside a time where you and your husband can talk privately. Each of you complete this sentence on a note card: "I experience the most sexual pleasure with you when . . ." Then exchange note cards. What happens next is up to the two of you.

_____

_____

_____ ■

♥ 5. Go back through the previous four days. Consider the gifts God wants you to open and the Scriptures we've discussed. List at least four opinions that God has about sex.

_____

_____

_____ ■

We pray that your heart has opened wide and that your spiritual eyes have seen God's perspective from His Word. We know you don't desire to copy the behavior and customs of this world's view of sexuality; you long to let God transform you into a new wife by changing the way you think (Romans 12:2, our paraphrase). Because this is your desire, you'll be excited about what you will learn in Day 5.

DAY 5

The Secret Place: Know the Truth

When Juli or Linda (or you) have an opinion, it's just that—an opinion. But when God has an opinion, it's called something else: truth. His opinion isn't just one of many; it is the one opinion against which all other thoughts and ideas are measured.

This week you studied His truth about sex. Time and time again, we took you back to God's Word because this is where truth is recorded. Friend, our opinions about your marriage or sex life won't amount to a hill of beans if they are not based on truth. Contrary to what you see on television, learn in university, or read in books, truth is not relative. Truth is God's opinion. And His opinion needs to become our fact.

Today we want to highlight for you why God's Word is an indispensable power source in your life. Reading God's Word is great but meditating on it, memorizing it, and personalizing it back to God is life transforming! Romans 12:2 speaks God's truth. We love the way the New Living Translation makes this verse come alive:

> Don't copy the behavior and customs of this world, but let God transform you into a new person by changing the way you think. Then you will learn to know God's will for you, which is good and pleasing and perfect. (Romans 12:2 NLT)

Do you see? Do you understand this glorious promise? God desires to take the truth of His Word and literally cause a transformation in you and in your intimacy with your husband! How? By changing the way you think about sex. The way you change is by making God's opinions your perspective.

Both Juli and I have taken God's opinion from Scripture about sex and made it part of us. How can you do this? Today in The Secret Place:

1. Choose a Scripture that has leapt off the page to you and make it your project.

2. Meditate on your chosen Scripture; ask the Lord to specifically speak its truth to you.

3. Make your chosen Scripture personal by praying it back to God in your own words.

Heather chose Song of Solomon 5:16: "His mouth is full of sweetness. And he is wholly desirable. This is my beloved and this is my friend" (NASB).

Heather's personalized prayer to God went like this:

"Oh God, David's kisses are blah . . . and I can't say he is wholly desirable. I don't know how to change my thinking but I'm burning this verse into my heart and talking to You about it every day this week. Okay, I just had a positive thought about his words—David knows I don't feel good about my body and he tries to build me up. That is sweetness from his mouth. Thank you for showing me this. I ask You, Father, to change my perspective so I look at my husband as both my lover and my friend."

♥ 4. Hebrews 4:12 says that God's Word is powerful—it is "living and active" and it "judges the thoughts and attitudes of the heart." As you continue to mediate on your chosen passage, describe how you see the Word come alive inside you and expose attitudes that previously had been hidden.

_____

_____

_____ ∎

The more of God's truth that you press down inside you, the more transformed you will be! We pray you will take this challenge seriously. When you do the work of memorizing God's living Word you can rest assured that He will change you into a new wife.

♥ 5 .Based on what you have studied this week, write a letter from God to you expressing what He desires for you to have in your sexual relationship with your husband.

_____

_____

_____

_____

_____

_____

_____

_____

_____ ∎

Making Truth Stick

What were your thoughts after the last lesson, God's Got an Opinion? We hope you were encouraged and thought, *I want to do whatever it takes to grow and have an amazing sex life. I long to know God's blessing over my marriage!* Maybe your thoughts were more like, *We're so far from the picture you painted of sexual intimacy that there is just no way I could see sex like that.* There is a reason why truth doesn't always "stick" when you read or hear it.

You may have discovered that your hang-ups and issues around sex come from your background or upbringing. At one level, you are right. How sex was addressed (or not) in your home, past sexual experiences, and traumas all contribute to your mindset about sex. However, there is something—or someone—else that keeps you from embracing God's truth. His name is Satan.

Let us assure you, we do not belong to the "There's a demon behind every bush" Bible teachers club. But the truth is: nowhere have we seen spiritual warfare more evident than in sexuality.

Why is Satan out to defeat you about sex?

Why does he want to keep God's truth from sticking to you?

Why does he care about your intimacy?

As you learned last week, sexual intimacy between a husband and wife is a holy picture of Christ and His church. God Almighty created the act of sex as a representation of the longing, the unity, the intimacy of Jesus Christ and His people. Satan's attack on sexuality

CHAPTER FOUR

THEME:

Your sexuality involves a spiritual battle between truths and lies.

THEME VERSE:

"...the one who is in you is greater than the one who is in the world."
(1 John 4:4b)

and marriage is about more than you and your husband. He aims to destroy, pollute, and disgustify (yes, we made that up) the precious and holy picture of oneness.

Because your marriage, your bedroom, your mind is a combat zone, your enemy works overtime to keep you from the truth.

Sex Is His Battlefield

When you hear the name C. S. Lewis, you probably think of the Chronicles of Narnia, but Lewis wrote many other amazing books. One of our favorites is *The Screwtape Letters*. Each chapter in this book gives us a fictional glimpse of the enemy's strategy to keep us from God's truth. If you listen carefully, perhaps you'll be able to hear Satan instructing his demon about you . . .

Do you see that nice Christian wife studying about pursuing passion? Last week she learned all about God's opinion on sex. Don't let God's truth stick! Confuse her mind. Fill her with doubts. Let her believe there is no hope for sex with her husband. Work hard to make sex disgusting, then she won't want to be unrestrained and abandoned. Create HUGE problems in this area. Let her think sex is the problem, not me. And specifically . . . Be sure to fill her mind with accusations:

You broke God's laws. You made so many wrong choices—you don't deserve to experience pleasure in sex.

Remember what he did to you—you're so defiled—you can never be healed. How could someone like you be an exciting lover—forget that.

What you and your husband did last night was wrong—you didn't feel right about it and you were on target. Such unbridled passion can't be from God.

In this week's teaching, we exposed five common lies that often keep women from embracing the truth of what God says about sex. To jog your memory, here are the five lies:

1. I'm not loved if I'm not desired.

2. I don't deserve a great sex life.

3. God doesn't care about my pain.

4. I'm too wounded to be healed.

5. I can fix problems with sexuality on my own.

It is very likely that you identified with at least one of these lies. In fact, you might have recognized all five of them in your thinking. The great news is that our Lord Jesus has defeated the lies and schemes of the evil one. Though Satan accuses and confuses, his schemes cannot stand against the power of the One who is Truth.

Do you believe that there is *really* a battle going on—a battle that you are part of—that affects your sexuality? There are parts of Scripture that we tune out even as we read them. Ephesians 6 is a "tune-out" passage. Right now, we ask you to tune in, read this out loud, and ask God to speak His truth into your heart.

> Finally, be strong in the Lord and in his mighty power. Put on the full armor of God so that you can take your stand against the devil's schemes. For our struggle is not against flesh and blood, but against the rulers, against the authorities, against the powers of this dark world and against the spiritual forces of evil in the heavenly realms. (verses 10–12)

This passage seems too "out there" to believe. So we tune out, check out, say ho hum, we'll let the "Lord of the Rings" handle the spiritual forces of wickedness in the heavenly places. We ask you, "Please don't tune out!" Just consider with us for a moment. Could this invisible warfare described in Scripture be playing out in your sexuality? Is it possible that spiritual forces are at work in the roots of insecurity, shame, selfishness, and anger that destroy intimacy between you and your husband? In the wake of rejection, fear, and pain, it's easy to look at the "enemy" on the other side of the bed and forget about the Enemy that has come to lie, steal, and destroy.

Embracing God's beautiful truth for your sexuality and intimacy means learning how to recognize and stand against Satan, who battles to keep you stuck in lies. At some level, maybe you are thinking, *I can't see it, and if I ignore it, maybe it won't really be there.* Ignoring it or minimizing it plays right into the adversary's hands because it keeps you from being alert and prepared.

These next five days, we are asking you to do some serious work, digging in the Word, looking in the mirror of truth, and getting on your knees. God's Word says that we must have a "battle mentality" and stand against the schemes of the evil one. This work will require time, dedication, and may be painful for you. But, our friend, your Beloved promises to be with you every step and He promises that He comes with healing and victory in His wings.

DAY 1
The Profile of a Liar

B e self-controlled and alert. Your enemy the devil prowls around like a roaring lion looking for someone to devour. (1 Peter 5:8)

In a battle, there are opposing forces. In this heavenly battle, God, the angelic host, and those on earth in His army are one force. Satan, the demonic angels, and those on earth in Satan's army are the opposing force. An army seeks to understand the opponent . . . do you understand yours? How would you describe Satan? What do you imagine him looking like and sounding like? Is he red with horns? Does his voice hiss like a snake? Although your Bible doesn't have a literal drawing or photograph of your enemy, it does sketch a profile of his character.

♥ 1. Read John 8:44; John 17:15; and John 12:31. How does each of these passages describe Satan?

_____

_____

_____ ∎

God's Word not only paints a picture of your enemy's character, it tells in detail his evil plans.

♥ 2. What does each of these passages say about your enemy's plans?

Matthew 4:1–3

_____

_____

_____ ∎

Revelation 12:9–10

_____

_____

_____ ∎

1 Peter 5:8

_____

_____

_____ ∎

Not a pretty picture. Satan is wicked, he is powerful, he has authority here on earth, and he has you in his sights. He will deceive, accuse, destroy, and murder—he's playing for keeps. Let us be perfectly clear. Satan has declared war in your marriage. He has set out to destroy you. How does he destroy?

He is the *accuser*. "You blew it! You don't deserve intoxicating intimacy!"

He is the *liar*. "Remember all of the times you've tried to get over your past? God's just not big enough to help you."

He is a *thief*. "How could you call yourself a good Christian and allow yourself to enjoy such earthy pleasure?"

He is *wicked*. "Your husband doesn't deserve sex. Just think of how insensitive he is."

He is a *tempter*. "You're only talking to him online. It's not like you are having an affair … yet."

He is a *destroyer*. "You have no hope. Your efforts and dreams to build a marriage will be fruitless. Give it up now!"

♥ 3. Ask God to reveal lies you have believed. Write a paragraph describing how your adversary speaks lies into your marriage and your sexuality.

_____

_____

_____ ■

♥ 4. Write your own paraphrase of 1 Peter 5:8 here. If you really believed this verse, what would look different in your intimacy with your husband?

_____

_____

_____ ■

♥ 5. Write a prayer to God asking Him to show you this week how to fight in this battle.

_____

_____

_____ ■

DAY 2

House of Thoughts

You may know the story in Matthew 16 where Jesus tells His disciples that He will soon be tortured and killed. Peter, one of Jesus' most devoted disciples, empathetically wanted to spare Him from the agony of what He was foretelling.

Peter took him aside and began to rebuke him. "Never, Lord!" he said. "This shall never happen to you!"

To you and me, Peter's words sound like a pep talk from a caring friend. But Jesus had the spiritual discernment to hear them differently. Read how He responded to Peter.

Get behind me, Satan! You are a stumbling block to me; you do not have in mind the things of God, but the things of men. (verse 23)

Jesus calls one of His best friends Satan! Peter must have been insulted, confused, and hurt. He just wanted to keep bad things from happening to his Master. Jesus knew the enemy well and recognized his lies immediately, even from the mouth of His friend.

We must be aware that Satan's lies can sound friendly and even more comfortable than the truth. How is this possible? Lies from the enemy settle down and take root in our own thoughts. The five lies we discussed in the session have power in your marriage once they have taken residence in your own thoughts.

The devious schemes of the devil have become so familiar that they sound friendly and not foreign. Satan has tremendous power in the lies you believe about sexuality! Each of us, based on personality and experience, are vulnerable to unique lies of the enemy. He knows where you are weak.

GETTING PERSONAL WITH *Juli*

Even though I grew up in a stable, Christian home and I was basically a "good girl" before marriage, I still brought sexual baggage and lies into marriage. One of the lies I believed for many years is that God created sex basically for my husband's pleasure, not mine. For a variety of reasons, sex was physically painful for me for the first several years of marriage. I started dreading and avoiding it. When Mike and I did have sex, I often felt like it was all about pleasing him. Satan used these circumstances to cause me to dread and resent Mike's advances. I became so resentful and frustrated that sex became a wedge between us. It wasn't until I started studying, teaching, and writing on the topic that I realized I had bought a lie. God's design is for both a husband and wife to be blessed by sex.

♥ 1. So, do you know the areas where you are vulnerable to the enemy's attacks? Is there a specific word or string of thoughts about sex that is an area of weakness?

_____

_____

_____

_____

_____

_____ ■

Satan's power is insidious and masterful because the lies have become your own thoughts, reinforced by your experience. They can feel more true than

the truth, and yet the enemy can oppress you through your own thoughts. You've heard Proverbs 23:7: "As a wife thinks in her heart, so is she" (our wording of NASB). In other words, the essence of who you are is in your thought life.

> It is difficult to discern the areas of oppression in our lives. After all, these are our thoughts, our attitudes, our perceptions—we justify and defend our thoughts with the same intensity with which we justify and defend ourselves.—Francis Frangipane[1]

The essence of who you are sexually and how you approach intimacy with your husband is in your thought life. To the extent the enemy has infiltrated your thinking, God's truth about sex will remain on the pages of your Bible and never make it to your bedroom!

You might not have a friend like Peter whispering Satan's lies in your ear. The enemy's voice may be your own thoughts. Once you have accepted his lie, he has a platform and power to taunt you and tempt you. The battle begins and ends with your thoughts!

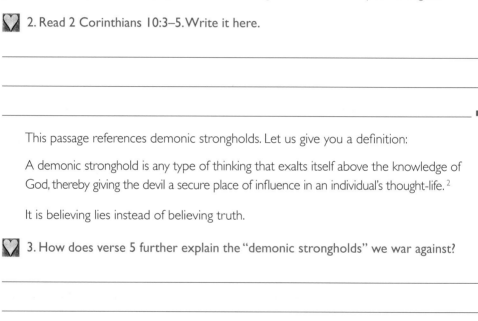 2. Read 2 Corinthians 10:3–5. Write it here.

_____

_____

_____ ▪

This passage references demonic strongholds. Let us give you a definition:

> A demonic stronghold is any type of thinking that exalts itself above the knowledge of God, thereby giving the devil a secure place of influence in an individual's thought-life. [2]

It is believing lies instead of believing truth.

3. How does verse 5 further explain the "demonic strongholds" we war against?

_____

_____

_____ ▪

Our friend, each of us has areas of our thinking about sex that potentially give the enemy strongholds of lies. They have become so familiar and have been reinforced so many times that we don't recognize they are the weapons of one who deceives and destroys! It's time to get specific about how Satan's lies have taken residence in your thoughts.

(Linda) My friend Kayla is a beautiful pastor's wife, with a loving husband and four children. She grew up with a father who went from mistress to mistress, always a younger and more beautiful version. The wife was to bear children and keep the home; the pretty young things were for his pleasure. As I shared with Kayla about Satan and his deceiving ways, she quickly saw lies the enemy had burned into her thoughts. Lies like: The seductress has power, the wife has none. Purity has no power. The way God created men is wrong.

I will never forget Kayla on her knees asking the Lord to forgive her for believing lies about men and sexuality. Her words of repentance poured out like a flowing river. Later she wrote me this email:

> *I am marinating in the truths you shared, trusting God with the growing capacity to overlay this new template of truth over hundreds (possibly thousands) of past hurts and memories that have rendered me emotionally crippled and spiritually stagnant.*

> *The revelation that, in my pain and deception, I have transposed and inverted men as the enemy, not the devil, has forever changed the nature of the battle. Lust and sexual brokenness now have a new face. I now know that Satan wears the masks of men, and men are not the enemy. This revelatory truth has set me free from the ball and chain of the worst battle I have encountered.*

4. Read 2 Corinthians 10:5 once more. What does it mean to you to take every thought (about your sexuality) captive to make it obedient to Christ?

_____

_____

_____

5. What specific lies and thoughts about your sexuality is God asking you to take captive today?

_____

_____

_____

6. Oh, how we need His discernment to recognize and rebuke the enemy's lies that come in the form of our own beliefs! Write a prayer to the Lord asking Him to reveal the lies in your own thoughts about your sexuality and intimacy with your husband.

_____

_____

_____

_____

DAY 3

It's All about the Man of Truth (Greater Is He Who Is in You!)

The four Gospels (Matthew, Mark, Luke, and John) record Jesus saying seventy-eight times, "I tell you the truth!" He has come to tell you the truth about your marriage and your sexuality. Remember the truths you studied last week about sex? Read them out loud:

God says that sex is designed to create intimate knowing between my husband and me.

God says that sex is a picture of the spiritual intimacy He desires with me.

God says that sex is a gift to bring me and my husband exquisite pleasure.

What you have just read is God's truth, His opinion about your sexual intimacy. His truth is specific and trustworthy. God's enemy Satan doesn't just make up lies randomly because he has nothing better to do. Have you ever noticed that he hasn't tried to convince you that the sky is green or that chocolate tastes bad? His lies and schemes always have a purpose. At the very core of every lie he whispers and every truth he distorts is the mother of all lies. Here it is:

GOD IS NOT TRUSTWORTHY

Living out of either the truth or a lie depends upon more than *what* you believe but upon *whom* you believe. Your adversary is not just interested in getting you to believe lies for the sake of lies. His ultimate goal is for you to doubt *Truth*—not the concept, the person.

The Lord Jesus does not just *like* truth. He doesn't just *speak* truth. He *is* truth (John 14:6)! Everything about Him is true. Many people try to kick out the lies from their mind and they fail. Only Truth can save you from a lie. And the Truth is Jesus Christ.

As you have been learning, Satan's schemes are crafty and subtle, twisting truth with lies. Let's revisit his encounter with the first lady in the garden of Eden.

♡ 1. Read again Genesis 2:16–17 and 3:1–7. How did Satan plant doubts in Eve's mind about God's trustworthiness and goodness?

_____

_____

_____ ■

♥ 2. Who did Satan tell Eve to trust instead of God?

_____

_____

_____ ■

Satan is deliberate in his attempt to dismantle each one of God's truths. He wants sex in your marriage to create conflict, not unity. He wants you to see it as carnal and nasty, not as a beautiful illustration of God's love and holiness. He will show you that the power of sex is used to cause pain, not pleasure. Most of all, **He wants you to doubt God's design for sex. He wants to tell you that God does not have your best interests in mind!**

♥ 3. Yesterday, we asked you to begin identifying specific lies about your sexuality that the enemy is assaulting you with. Write the lie or lies here.

_____

_____

_____ ■

♥ 4. How is each lie ultimately a lie about God's trustworthiness?

_____

_____

_____ ■

You have read I Peter 5:8–9 this week. It paints a frightening picture of Satan as a roaring lion, seeking to devour you. If that doesn't make you just a bit scared, check your pulse. Battling this enemy is scary. Some are devoured by him. Yet being prepared for battle and being afraid are two different things.

♥ 5. Now read I Peter 5:7, the verse right before the "roaring lion." Write it here.

_____

_____

_____ ■

While Jesus tells you to stand firm against the enemy, He also tells you that He cares deeply for you. And He tells you exactly what to do about your anxiety—cast it on Him.

You can throw the whole weight of your anxiety on Him for you are His personal concern. It matters to Him concerning you. Have a battle mentality, be on the alert, your enemy, the devil prowls about like a roaring lion, looking for someone to devour. But resist him, stand firm in your faith! (1 Peter 5:7–9 our translation, with a little of the Phillips included)

Your cares, anxieties—all that troubles you about sexual intimacy with your husband is of deep concern to your Abba Father. He cares for you affectionately and He cares for you watchfully. While you sleep tonight, He will be awake praying for you. Because His love for you—for your marriage—is so deep, He longs for you to throw all your anxious care onto His strong shoulders.

How do you throw your anxiety about your sexual intimacy onto Him? We'll let Maureen tell you how she cast a huge care on the Lord.

The abortions I had were like a noose around my neck. I would take a step forward in freedom and I would hear, "Remember what you did . . . you can't be free." It was like a revelation when I realized the enemy was taunting me with those words. I longed to hurl all my anxiety, my guilt, on the Lord. So I took a rock, went out for a walk, and named the rock with my anxiety. "Rock, your name is abortion." I told the Lord I couldn't carry the weight of it any longer and I hurled the rock as far as I could . . . away from me, onto Him. My shoulders felt lighter, my burden was on HIS strong shoulders. And whenever the Accuser would throw his taunting words of guilt at me, I would say, "God says my sin is cast into the depths of the sea and that He put up a 'no fishing' sign. So get behind me, Satan. I won't listen to your lies."

♥ 6. Outside your home, you can find a rock. Spend some time with the Lord alone, telling Him about the "rock" you have been carrying. Does it have a name? Throw the

rock as far away as you can as a symbol of trusting the Lord with your cares—cast them on Him.

You have a choice today. You've heard, read, and studied what God says about sex and you have learned about Satan's intentions to destroy truth. So we ask you, whom do you trust? We understand that the lies can feel safe and comfortable. If your childhood taught you that sex is painful, traumatic, destructive, and exploitive, grasping the truth that God's design for sex is beautiful is a huge leap! The ugly message from Satan feels true and safe. Maybe your heart is pounding as you read these words . . . your Savior is asking you a question: *Will you trust Me, precious one? For I have come that you might have life.*

DAY 4

Getting Dressed for Battle

As you have wrestled with the lies you believe this week, has it become a reality that Jesus is greater than Satan? Although our enemy has great power, he is a defeated foe. God, in His sovereignty, allows Satan's lies to come against us. Yet, Satan does not have the power to defeat us. You do not stand alone in your battle against the enemy! God so desires you, His precious daughter, to know how to fight against lies that He even tells you how to dress for battle.

1. Read Ephesians 6:10–12. Who do these verses say you have to be protected against?

_____

_____

_____ ■

2. Read Ephesians 6:13–18. Write a paragraph describing your fighting garments.

_____

_____

_____

_____ ■

We know all of this sounds a little otherworldly. It is! But it is also just as real as the laundry piled in your bathroom and the roof over your head. God wants you to be equipped in this world to stand against the invisible spiritual forces that fight against you.

Perhaps you are wondering, *Okay, Linda and Juli. I get that there is a spiritual battle. I can even see the lies I have believed. But how do you actually put this stuff into practice throughout daily life?* We have asked that same question. Here are three very practical steps you can use to confront the enemy's lies in your marriage:

Step 1: **SPEAK** the lie.

Step 2: **HOLD UP** the shield of faith in your left hand—"I trust my Lord Jesus Christ. He is Truth!"

Step 3: **PROCLAIM** the truth with the Sword of the Spirit in your right hand.

♥ 3. Read Matthew 4:1–10. Identify how Jesus:

Spoke the lie.

_____

_____

_____ ▪

Held up the shield of faith.

_____

_____

_____ ▪

Proclaimed truth with the Sword of the Spirit, which is the Word of God.

_____

_____

_____ ▪

    Tamara was sexually abused from the time she was very young. Sex was dirty, disgusting, gross, and vile. Now she was getting married. She needed to fight against the lies and for God's truth.

    How Tamara fought her fight:

I wanted everything about marriage with this man I loved except sex . . . never sex. I was shocked to learn God's opinion and to realize that, because of my deep pain about sex, I had believed a lie. So I asked God to show me how to fight the enemy's lies to me.

First, I said the lie out loud: "I'm believing that because of my past, I can't enjoy sex. I can't be pure."

Second, I declared that I wanted to believe in Christ and His truth about my sexuality.

Third, I proclaimed Scripture right at Satan like Jesus did. "Therefore, if any woman is in Christ, she is a new creature; the old things passed away; behold, new things have come" (2 Corinthians 5:17 NASB).

*"God, I want only Your new thoughts, new beliefs about sex, to be part of me. I thank
You that You say new things have come. Let it be true in my marriage. Show me how
to live this with my new husband!"*

Our friend Judy Dunagan shares wise advice about how to fight the enemy as a couple:

*I have found when couples are facing a fierce battle, that reading Scripture out loud
(hopefully together) is a powerful weapon. Rick and I memorized Psalm 91 during
a severe storm in our marriage and often Rick would pray it over me when the
battle was raging. I think Psalm 91 is one of the key "warfare" passages of Scripture,
speaking of our authority over the lion and the cobra.*

*Another tool that is powerful for marriages in the battle is praying out loud together.
Many couples don't know where to start or how to pray on the armor and so they don't.
I know in my own journey that having a written prayer, full of Scripture, can be so helpful
when the battle is especially fierce against my marriage or family.*

Throughout the past few days, you have been asking your Abba Father to help you
discern the lies the enemy tells you about your marriage and your sexuality. You have written
them down, prayed about them, and asked for truth to confront them. Does it encourage
you, friend, to know that Jesus is interceding on your behalf even now (see Hebrews 7:25)?

Taking the next step to hold up the shield of faith and proclaim truth depends upon
knowing the truth deep within your heart. In the passages you just studied, you saw Jesus
defeat Satan with truth by reciting Scripture. Ephesians 6:17 says that proclaiming truth from
God's Word is like holding a sword that deals a blow to your enemy. But to stand on truth,
you must know it.

4. Write down three Scripture passages that you can use to stand against the specific
lies to which you are most vulnerable. We have given you a few examples from other
women but we want you to seek the Word of God for yourself.

_____

_____

_____

_____

_____

_____

_____

_____

DAY 5

The Secret Place: Worship!

This week, your time in the secret place is about worship. Worship is one of the most powerful ways to develop intimacy with God and tear down the lies of the enemy. "In warfare, worship is a wall around the soul."[3]

Most Christians think of worship as the songs they sing on Sunday morning in church. Corporate worship is a beautiful celebration and offering of praise to the King of kings. But private worship, the type that occurs in The Secret Place, is essential to your victory in claiming truth. When you worship, you are holding fast to the shield of faith, placing your trust in the Lord. At the same time, you are proclaiming who Jesus is, thrusting the sword of truth into the enemy. While Scripture memorization renews your mind, worship is the language of loving God that allows truth to wash over your heart.

Here's a secret: Satan *hates* it when you worship the Lord! Read the following beautiful description of why praise is so effective against Satan.

In Psalm 22:3 we are told that God "inhabits the praises" of His people. This means that wherever there is adoration, reverence, and acceptable worship and praise, there He identifies and openly manifests His presence. And His presence always expels Satan. Satan cannot operate in the divine ambience. In short, Satan is allergic to praise, so where there is massive, triumphant praise, Satan is paralyzed, bound, and banished.—Paul Billheimer[4]

♥ 1. Put on worship music, kneel, and humbly ask the Lord to take you deeper into all it means to worship Him.

_____

_____

_____

_____

_____

♥ 2. This lesson has been about Making Truth Stick, so take the word TRUTH and express praise for who He is as TRUTH with these letters: (We've started but think you can add more!)

T—Truth, Trustworthy _____

R—Restorer, Renewer _____

U—Unbelievable, Upright _____

T—Tender, Teacher _____

H—Holy, Healer _____

♥ 3. Use some of the praise words from "TRUTH" and write out a prayer to your God thanking Him for who He is!

_____

_____

_____

_____ ■

♥ 4. Write a list of your "praises" to God for your sexual intimacy with your husband. We've started the list for you . . . keep it going!

_____

_____

_____ ■

I praise You for the gift of sex

I praise You that we can grow deeper in sexual intimacy

I praise You that You make all things new

I praise You for forgiveness

I praise You that You are the healer of my sexuality

I praise You that intoxicating sex is for my husband and me

We hope you will be excited about worshiping your God of TRUTH—so continue delighting in all He is and worshiping Him in spirit and in truth! Our friend Alaine said it well:

When I die, I don't want to be remembered as one who knew how to fight Satan,
I want to be remembered as a worshiper of my God!
Amen!

What Kind of Love Are You Making?

CHAPTER FIVE

THEME:

Sexual differences present you with a secret choice: Will I be a servant lover or a selfish lover?

THEME VERSE:

"Don't be selfish; don't try to impress others. Be humble, thinking of others (your husband) as better than yourselves."
(Philippians 2:3 NLT)

Wife: "After an exhausting day of chasing after kids, working during their naps, and playing housewife, it's finally time to rest! I barely fall asleep when Romeo comes to bed after midnight and grabs at me. How can he be so insensitive and selfish? Am I just a body to him?"

Husband: "I've been working so many hours lately. Meetings keep running over and deadlines pressing in. I just want to be home with my wife. All I can think of is her body. I finally get home to find her asleep. She won't mind if I wake her up. I bet she's been waiting all day to see me."

Wife: "Seriously! He wakes me up for this! Naturally, I told him to forget it. If he wants me in bed, he needs to start by showing me love during the day. What does he think I do all day? Sit around waiting for him, thinking about sex?"

Husband: "I should have known she'd respond like this. Why do I even try?"

Does this sound familiar? Would you be surprised to learn that this type of encounter has been going on for centuries? This is actually a modern day adaptation of Smokin' Hot Mama and her husband. The differences between these two lovers threatened to spoil their intimacy and caused the only conflict we see in *Song of Solomon*.

Things haven't changed much since Solomon recorded how different he and his bride were. You and your husband are still different sexually, and those differences threaten to destroy intimacy between you. You have questions about God's design. A young wife named Nicole did too.

Lord, why did You make men and women so different sexually? My husband and I have different sexual appetites; what arouses him turns me off, and we even use different words to communicate about sex. Is this a cruel joke? It seems as if You have dangled the promise of pleasure and oneness out for us to see, but we can't taste it because we are too different to be able to please each other!

Have you, like Nicole, ever wondered why God made you and your husband so different? Have your attempts to be sexually fulfilled resulted in conflict rather than unity?

Get ready for a new concept. We want to challenge you with a radical statement! **Sexual differences between you and your husband can be a powerful source of unity.** Sound crazy? Just be patient and bear with us. This is important.

The very things that you fight about in the bedroom:

- How often to have sex
- How much foreplay
- Are sex toys okay
- What words to use
- A scary new sexual something

. . . all of these things can flip from destroying intimacy to actually taking you to a deeper oneness.[1] It's going to take some work and determination to get there but we think you're up for the task!

DAY 1

No, God Didn't Make a Mistake!

Imagine that you and your husband live in sexual utopia. You always want to have sex at exactly the same time and same way that your husband wants it. Every initiation is met with an eager response. There is never any conflict about foreplay, being too tired, giving each other pleasure, or trying something new in bed because your desires are always exactly the same. How fantastic would that be? It would be almost like the sex portrayed in movies—what a great love life!

God, the creative Creator, certainly could have made sex that way. He could have created man and woman to be exactly the same sexually. But He didn't. In fact, He intentionally made us vastly different. Read how wives say these differences play out in their marriages.

"I like lots of romance and nonsexual touching. He wants to get to the 'goal' right away."—Jasmine

"My husband really isn't interested in sex. When he is, it's a five-minute quickie. Oh, how I'd just love for him to want to enjoy my body!"—Jessie

"He is an 'every day is a good day for sex' man . . . twice a month would make me happy."—Nashonna

"He wants to prove he is a 'sexual superman' by having me orgasm two, three times. I'm happy with once. Why does it have to be a contest? Why can't we really make love?"—Cynthia

"My husband seems to always want to push the envelope in bed. I just like to enjoy the sweetness of being together."—Sonja

"All my husband needs is to see me naked for a few seconds and he's ready for action. It seems like it takes me hours to get my mind into being sexual. He gets so frustrated with me but I just can't switch gears like he does."—Carly

Did God make a mistake with these couples? Did He mess up the master design of sex by making a husband and wife so diverse? Does He sit up in heaven and laugh that we can't seem to please each other?

Basic Differences

MEN	WOMEN
Sex leads to feelings of love	Feelings of love leads to sex
Quickly aroused and satisfied	Slowly aroused and satisfied
Best part of sex is **release** tension—the goal	Best part of sex is **buildup** of tension—the journey
Wants immediate direct stimulation in one place	Wants to be touched everywhere delaying direct stimulation
Wants sex in order to relax	Must relax in order to have sex
Aroused visually	Aroused by emotions / sensations
Sexual prime late teens, early 20s	Sexual prime 30s and 40s
Desire dependent on constant hormones	Desire dependent on changing hormones
Capable of single orgasm	Capable of multiple and varied orgasms

Remember that even before sin entered the garden of Eden, Adam and Eve had primary sexual differences in the way God created them. God declared His creation of man and woman "very good" and this very good included your sexual differences. It is hard to fathom but the differences between you and your husband are what can create the very deepest *yada* intimacy.

You might be thinking *Okay, Juli and Linda. I want to believe what you are telling me but you just don't understand how frustrating it is. I desperately want a great sex life, but my husband and I are never on the same page. Sex is driving such a wedge between us that we can't even talk about it. How in the world can our differences actually bring us closer together?*

Here's the deal. God's design for sex is *not* just for immediate exquisite pleasure (although He is all for that). But God has a much more beautiful gift of intimacy for you and your husband to open than what the world says sex is about. Here's the catch. It requires a different kind of love.

Sex is designed to be more than an expression of love between a husband and wife. It is also the refining fire of love. It tests and teaches a willing man and woman to reach beyond their natural desires and learn what servant love really is.

The world knows only of a love that feels good. We are born with the natural response to "love" those who meet our physical and emotional needs. This kind of natural love is essentially self-love. It really says, "I love the way you make me feel."

If your husband had the same sex drive as you, if he liked to kiss and be touched all over the same way you do, frankly, loving him wouldn't cost you much.

You already know how to love your husband with natural, selfish love. It's easy to please him when he's pleasing you. But do you know the secret of loving him when it's a "bad husband day"? Do you know how to respond to him sexually when it's the very last thing on earth you feel like doing? *This* is the kind of love that God wants to develop in you and your husband. And He just might be using your sexual differences as the training ground.

In contrast to selfish love, God's love for us is unconditional, unchanging, and steadfast. We call this servant love. Instead of always asking, "What's in it for me?" servant love asks, "How can I bless my husband?"

♥ 1. How have you been tempted to love your husband sexually only with this type of selfish love?

_____

_____

_____ ∎

♥ 2. Read 1 Corinthians 13:4–8a and paraphrase this beautiful description of servant love.

_____

_____

_____

_____ ∎

GETTING PERSONAL WITH *Linda*

I took the beautiful statements about servant love in 1 Corinthians 13 and made them a personal prayer to the Lord. The first day I took the thought of love being patient. It went like this:

Today, Lord, how can my love be patient? I want to: Give the grace I give to a friend to Jody. Get behind his eyeballs and see the today of life as he sees it. Be as understanding of his weaknesses as I was the first year of our marriage.

♥ 3. Choose two phrases from 1 Corinthians 13 and personalize them to God about your marriage like Linda did.

_____

_____

_____

_____

_____ ■

♥ 4. How do you think God can use sexual differences between a husband and wife to teach them servant love?

_____

_____

_____ ■

♥ 5. What differences have caused the most tension and distress in your sexual relationship?

_____

_____

_____ ■

♥ 6. Complete these sentences:

If I respond to our sexual differences with selfish love, I will . . .

_____

_____

_____ ■

If I respond to our sexual differences with servant love, I will . . .

_____

_____

_____ ■

The title of this chapter is "What Kind of Love Are You Making?" The way you respond to the differences between you and your husband will answer this question. Are you a selfish lover or a servant lover?

 7. How specifically can you make a secret choice to allow those differences to teach you to love your husband as 1 Corinthians 13 explains?

_____

_____

_____

_____ ∎

DAY 2

Humble Pie Is an Aphrodisiac

Around the world, people believe they have discovered the perfect product for arousal. Throughout the centuries, oats have been considered an aphrodisiac. Maybe you've heard, "That guy is just sowing his wild oats." In China, hippopotamus snout is a sought-after libido enhancer, but we doubt if any is available at Walmart. Perhaps the most commonly talked about aphrodisiac is oysters, though green M&Ms sound more appetizing to us than they do. We're not sure if they work, but what a great excuse to eat them.

With all the wives' tales and urban legends about aphrodisiacs, is there really a desire booster? We believe we have found one that actually works: *humility*. It may not be classified as an arousal agent, but we're convinced it supernaturally paves the way for unity through differences.

Is there is any encouragement from belonging to Christ? Any comfort from his love? Any fellowship together in the Spirit? Are your hearts tender and compassionate? Then make me truly happy by agreeing wholeheartedly with each other, loving one another, and working together with one mind and purpose. Don't be selfish; don't try to impress others. Be humble, thinking of others as better than yourselves. Don't look out only for your own interests, but take an interest in others, too. (Philippians 2:1–4 NLT)

Did you know this passage is about how to build unity? And it even applies to *sexual* unity.

1. What do you think "agreeing wholeheartedly, having the same love, spirit, and purpose" means when it comes to your sexual intimacy?

_____

_____

_____ ■

Here's our paraphrase of Philippians 2:1–4:

If God has been good to you in any way, say "thank you" by seeking unity with each other. How do you do this? Stop pursuing your own agenda! This begins with humility and unselfish actions.

Today we want to take a closer look at Paul's instruction for us to "in humility consider others better than yourselves." We believe that this is a _key_ to transforming the way you approach differences in the bedroom. _Differences divide when we become proud and self-righteous._

 2. Have you ever considered your husband's sexuality as _better_ than your own? If so, how?

_____

_____

_____ ■

From the time we were little girls, we teased boys with limericks and jokes like these:

Girls rule, boys drool.
Girls are cute, boys are not. Girls are sweet, boys just rot.
Girls know everything; boys just don't know it yet.

And as girls become women, they get a bit more caustic. "God made men before women because you always make a rough draft before the final masterpiece."

Yes, boys are armed with their share of comebacks and put-downs for the girls. The underlying message of the "battle of the sexes" is that my approach to life and relationship is better than my husband's. This opinion plays out dramatically in sexual differences. The vast majority of women (including us) have been stuck in the thinking that a woman's sexuality is _better—more authentic, more mature, more dignified, and more spiritual_ than a man's.

♥ 3. What are some of the derogatory things you have heard women say about male sexuality?

_____

_____

_____ ■

♥ 4. What impact do you think these types of comments have on a husband?

_____

_____

_____ ■

Think about the last time you and your husband disagreed about something sexually. Maybe you approached him for sex and he rejected you. Or maybe he suggested something too risky for your taste and it completely turned you off. What was the internal monologue going on inside you? What thoughts ran through your mind? Most likely, you thought about all the reasons why your husband was insensitive, selfish, or even perverted. Bottom line: you ruminated about how your approach was right and your husband's was wrong.

This is key for you to understand: it is not the sexual differences in your relationship that are causing the conflict. *It is the way you and your husband react to those differences.* Pride and self-righteousness are the natural way to respond and will always lead to conflict.

♥ 5. How has pride or self-righteousness played out in your approach to your husband's sexuality?

_____

_____

_____ ■

♥ 6. What attitudes and experiences keep you from valuing your husband's sexuality more highly than your own?

_____

_____

_____ ■

We know that what Paul wrote in Philippians sounds crazy, particularly if you apply it to sex. However, these verses tell you how to make servant love!

♥ 7. Read Philippians 2:2–5 out loud to God. Ask Him if there has been a "my way is the right way" in your attitude or actions. If so, seek your God on how you can move toward humility.

a. Do you need to ask the Lord to forgive you?

b. Do you need to ask your husband to forgive you?

c. How can you show your husband you are growing a new attitude?

Describe how you are going to take an action step.

_____

_____

_____ ■

DAY 3

Getting behind Your Husband's Eyeballs

Yesterday, we learned from the apostle Paul that differences divide us when we become proud. Humility paves the way for servant love and unity. Today we want to center in on two very convicting verses about selfishness.

Do nothing out of selfish ambition or vain conceit . . . each of you should look not only to your own interests (or needs), but also to the interests of others (your husband). (Philippians 2:3–4)

Differences divide when we become self-absorbed. The average couple becomes so frustrated with their sexual differences that they literally lose the ability to understand how their spouse thinks or feels about sex. Paul's teaching in Philippians says that we cannot be unified until we lay down our selfishness and consider what our husband needs.

♥ 1. Write a paragraph describing what it would look like for you to "look to your husband's sexual interests."

_____

_____

_____ ■

To help you understand why sex is such a big deal to guys, we want to encourage you to grasp and affirm God's intentional design for your husband's sexuality. The following four questions might challenge your perspective.

1. *Why does everything have to be about the penis?*

Why? Because his penis is the core of his masculinity . . . it defines who he is as a man. A woman's body shouts she is feminine. Her monthly period says, "You are being prepared to be a mother." Her body contorts to hold a growing baby. Her breasts swell with milk to nourish her child. Her body declares . . . you are mother, you are feminine. What does a man have that declares his masculinity? One thing: his prowess as a lover. The taking of his wife. How? With his rigid, engorged penis. God created the penis as man's symbol of masculinity. Why is Viagra a multimillion-dollar business? Because the male organ not swelling is a sign to him that he is not masculine. He can't be who God created him to be, the aggressor who woos and wins his wife.

2. *Why is sex so important to my husband?*

The hormone that regulates sexual drive in both a man and a woman is testosterone. The average man has twenty times more testosterone than his wife! This is a biological reason why sex is often on his mind. However, contrary to what many women think, sex isn't just a biological drive for men. Many men experience sex as the primary way of connecting and communicating emotionally with their wives.

> *In a man's body, the sexual organs are external and given for one purpose and that is for intercourse. So, it is a huge part of his manhood. When he has a bad day, sex is needed. When he has a good day, sex is desired. It is the giving and receiving of the sexual union that drives men to protect us, care for us, love us, and even die for us. His organs are "outside" the body. They are external.*—Sally Meredith[2]

3. *Why does he only want to be touched in one place?*

There is a biological reason. All sixteen of a man's sexual glands are located in one place—yep, you guessed it. As a woman, we are aroused by his touch on our shoulders, back, running his hand between our breasts, around our breasts, skimming his fingers all over our body. But for him, sexual excitement isn't all over. It is in one place. It is God's design.

4. *Why does he look at women's bodies?*

The Lord created your husband to be sexually stimulated by the sight of a naked female body. This is His design and it is to be a gift for you! God designed your husband to be absolutely captivated by the sight of you without clothes. The draw was created to be so great that his desire for you completely overlooked your stretch marks, wrinkles, or cellulite. God also designed your husband to want to be naked with you often. Your husband's sexual desire (and his desire to get you naked) causes his thoughts to return to you over and over again throughout the years of marriage. He can't go very long without needing to touch you. What a gift!

GETTING PERSONAL WITH Juli

I've always been a bit squeamish about talking about sex. No, really, I have! So discussing my needs and Mike's needs was not easy. One thing that really helped was to read good books on sex together, out loud. That way, the author could say words like "penis" and "orgasm" and I didn't have to. Then, Mike or I could just say, "I feel just like that." Here are a few books that we recommend for you and your husband to read together.

Intimate Issues
by Linda Dillow and Lorraine Pintus
Intimacy Ignited
by Jody and Linda Dillow, Peter and Lorraine Pintus
No More Headaches
by Juli Slattery
The Gift of Sex
by Cliff and Joyce Penner
The Way to Really Love Your Wife
by Cliff and Joyce Penner
Celebration of Sex
by Douglas Rosenau

Friend, we beg you, don't allow Satan's distortion of male sexuality to blind you to what God has magnificently created.

Think again about the "no selfishness" verse: "Do nothing out of selfish ambition or vain conceit . . . each of you should look not only to your own interests (or needs), but also to the interests of others (your husband)." (Philippians 2:3–4)

♡ 2. What are your needs that you must temporarily "lay down" in order to understand and value your husband's interests in the bedroom?

_____

_____

_____

_____

_____

_____

_____ ∎

What God through His Word is asking you to do is not easy, nor is it natural. However, He is not asking you to do anything that He has not Himself done.

♡ 3. Read Philippians 2:5–8 and paraphrase it in your own words.

_____

_____

_____

_____

_____

_____

_____ ∎

♥ 4. How might Jesus' example of humility and "emptying Himself" apply to how you respond to your husband's needs?

_____

_____

_____ ∎

A very important step to living out Philippians 2 is learning to be a good listener. We are not talking about the "How was your day, honey?" type of listening. We are referring to the listening that deeply wants to know your husband's needs. The listening that wants to understand his sexual temptations and vulnerabilities. And the listening that responds with empathy and a desire to fulfill him. This listening requires you to temporarily put aside your own needs, wants, and opinions for the expressed desire of becoming an authentic, servant lover.

Talking at this level about sexual needs can be intimidating for many couples. It can bring up pain from the past and can feel awkward. However, this is a vital step to becoming united rather than divided through differences.

♥ 5. Set up a time where you and your husband can be alone and unhurried. Tell him that you want to understand more about his sexual needs. You might even want to write him a letter expressing your desire if that is easier for you. During your time alone, ask him these questions:

- Is there anything you feel that I don't understand about your sexual needs?
- Can you tell me one thing I can do to become a better lover to you?

This is really important: whatever he says or doesn't say, just listen. Don't get defensive. Don't hit him with ten more questions. Just listen and thank him for being vulnerable. If he is comfortable with doing so, pray together that the Lord will help you become a better lover for your husband.

DAY 4
You've Got Needs Too!

Many women struggle with the challenge of considering and valuing their husband's needs. Their natural bent is to be selfish. Other women go to the opposite extreme and become selfless. In other words, their whole existence and their entire approach to sex is about meeting their husband's needs and ignoring their own. As altruistic as this may sound, it's not a healthy or biblical perspective. In fact, a wife who is completely selfless will create and enable selfishness in her husband.

Finding unity in differences is not just about understanding and pleasing your husband. Your needs are important too!

♥ 1. Read Philippians 2:4 and write it here.

_____

_____

_____ ■

♥ 2. What does this passage say about *your* interests or needs?

_____

_____

_____ ■

We have seen many wives resign themselves to the belief that God created sex primarily for the husband's fulfillment and pleasure. They understand their role as only one of service—bringing their husband pleasure in bed. Although this is a part of God's call to a wife, it is only a part. God created sex to be thoroughly enjoyed by both the husband *and* wife. Settling for a sex life that revolves around only one of them is a compromise of God's design and intention.

I (Juli) remember counseling a woman whose husband demanded sex three times a day, including once in the middle of the night and it wasn't a quickie in the dark. He wanted lights, mirrors, and sex toys. This woman understood her role as a godly wife as never saying no to her husband, regardless of how tired she was or how unreasonable his requests were. By obliging her husband sexually three times every day, she never encouraged her husband to grow as a sensitive, servant lover.

Some women have difficulty accepting that sexual pleasure is something good for them to pursue. It seems more godly or ladylike to just be a servant lover without allowing sexual feelings for themselves. This is not biblical or healthy for your marriage. As you are learning by studying Song of Solomon, God designed you to pursue sexual pleasure and oneness within marriage.

In chapter 1, we talked briefly about a man's need to feel competent and to believe that he is your hero. A very important part of that is being your hero in bed. His own pleasure will be short-lived and superficial if you are not also pleased.

Truth be told, women often don't understand their own sexuality. Becoming aroused and experiencing orgasm seems to be an allusive mystery. They don't understand themselves, so forget about trying to explain it to their husbands!

A huge roadblock for many women to becoming a SHM is this: great sex requires abandonment. You cannot be self-conscious, reserved, or controlled and experience passionate intimacy. Great lovers find a way to lose themselves in the experience of sexual pleasure and passion. Save your type-A, structured personality for spring-cleaning. When you walk into your bedroom, leave your inhibitions at the door. Keep your self-conscious ponderings to the therapist's office. Sexual intimacy is the time to be free.

The word *inhibit* means to restrain, to hinder, to prohibit, to check. Do women have an issue with inhibitions? We think the answer is yes. They want to be sexually free to provocatively delight the one they love but, instead of being abandoned, they are restrained.

 3. What do you think inhibits you from being free to express yourself sexually?

_____

_____

_____ ■

Many women ask us about how to enjoy pleasure in sex. Here are some of the most common questions:

"How do I relax enough to experience orgasm?"

"How do I get past feeling so self-conscious during sex? I think I would be too embarrassed if I just let myself go."

"I just can't get my mind into sex most of the time. My husband can usually tell when I'm a hundred miles away. Any suggestions?"

Imagine a road, a pathway, from one destination to another. The road begins with normal, everyday life and ends in amazing sexual pleasure. How do you get there? God has designed each woman, each couple with a pathway to sexual pleasure. There are different signposts along the way that you might be able to identify. Some of the signposts might include what you think about or sensations in your body. As you learn your unique pathway to pleasure, sexual intimacy will increasingly become a blessed gift. As you learn your husband's pathway to pleasure, you will become a skilled lover.

Your pathway to sexual pleasure involves your mind as much as it involves your body. In fact, your body is unlikely to respond sexually if your mind cannot be engaged.

Unfortunately, many women feel restrained in their thinking sexually. Somewhere along the pathway to pleasure, they hit roadblocks like these:

"Sex to me is so dirty and repulsive. My father sexually abused me for as long as I can remember. It is sick and I feel sick and sex is sick."

"I just can't be that vulnerable with my husband. I don't know how to trust him."

"What is my husband thinking? I wonder if he notices the cellulite on my hips."

"I can't get into this tonight. I've got too much on my mind."

Being free in your mind means replacing these "yield" or "stop" signs with a big, fat GO!!! You can do this by concentrating on your husband, your desire for him, or even reciting Scripture from SOS. Sex becomes even more intimate when you share the quest for the "pathway to pleasure" with your husband.

You and your husband need to work openly and honestly to find ways to bring both of you pleasure. We want you to grasp that understanding, valuing, and communicating your sexual needs to your husband is loving, biblical, and vital. And get this: your husband *cannot know what you want or need sexually unless you tell him!* We know how romantic it sounds to have a husband who intuitively knows exactly when and how to touch you. But it just doesn't happen.

Throughout Song of Solomon, we see SHM being assertive (not demanding) about her sexual needs and feelings. She made it clear to her husband what she desired and what was pleasing to her. This set her husband up for success. Listen to her use of imagery to tell Solomon she is filled with desire:

> Sustain me with raisin cakes, refresh me with apples, because I am lovesick.
> Let his left hand be under my head and his right hand embrace me. (Song 2:5–6 NASB)

SHM asks for sustenance to alleviate her lovesickness—raisin cakes and apples are the cure. Both are symbols of erotic love. Then she tells him exactly how to hold her. His left hand under her head to support her and his right hand embrace her. The Hebrew word *habaq*, translated here "to embrace," has the sense of "to fondle." Smokin' Hot Mama is free with her words, free to express how Solomon can please her sexually.

♥ 4. How does the SHM express her desire to her husband in the following verses?

a. 1:2

_____

_____

_____ ■

b. 3:4

_____

_____

_____ ■

c. 4:16

_____

_____

_____ ■

d. 7:10–8:3

_____

_____

_____ ∎

 5. Why does it promote unity for you to express and communicate your sexual needs to your husband?

_____

_____

_____ ∎

 6. Find a creative way to communicate to your husband what brings you sexual pleasure. Here are a few ideas:

- Write a poem describing what feels good to you about sex.

- Each of you write three things you really enjoy about your lovemaking and share them with each other. Then each write one thing that would give you added pleasure. Share these too.

- During an intimate time with your husband, place his hand over yours. Let your hand guide him over your body, teaching him where and how you want to be touched.

DAY 5

The Secret Place: Choosing Servant Love

The theme of this week's lesson is that every sexual difference provides the opportunity for you to become a servant lover. You will not embrace this message unless you place your faith in the fact that God can unite you through your differences if you trust Him. By choosing servant love instead of selfish love, you are using your power to build unity.

The Message has a beautiful paraphrase of 1 Corinthians 7:3–5 that speaks of choosing servant love:

Sexual drives are strong, but marriage is strong enough to contain them and provide for a balanced and fulfilling sexual life in a world of sexual disorder.

The marriage bed must be a place of mutuality—the husband seeking to satisfy his wife, the wife seeking to satisfy her husband. Marriage is not a place to "stand up for your rights." Marriage is a decision to serve the other, whether in bed or out.

Did you get that? Being a faithful wife is a decision to serve your husband, whether in bed or out. Have you ever thought of faithfulness to your husband as the decision to serve him, in the living room and the bedroom?

♥ 1. Spend time with the Lord personalizing this passage from 1 Corinthians 7 as a prayer to Him. Write your prayer here.

_____

_____

_____

_____

_____

_____ $Love$

_____ ■

♥ 2. Write three ways you can serve your husband in bed this week.

_____

_____

_____ ■

God wants to do more than change your thinking. He wants to transform the way you and your husband act toward each other. We trust that He has this week showed you at least one way to use your sexual differences to reach toward your husband with love and unity.

We began this week's study with a modern-day adaptation of the argument between the SHM and her husband. Read Song of Solomon 5:2–3 and you will see that both Solomon and SHM were thinking of their own needs. We see Solomon come home late at night (after midnight) and want to make love (verse 2). Then SHM makes up an excuse about how she can't possibly make love at this late hour (I'm all ready for bed and it would be too hard to put my dress back on and come open the door—verse 3). In other words, "Solomon, I want to sleep!" Now read Song of Solomon 5:4–16.

3. What choice did SHM make to become a servant lover through differences?

_____

_____

_____ ■

You have a choice to make about how you will respond to the sexual differences between you and your husband. You can stay in your own corner, dwelling on how your perspective is better than his. Or, like SHM, you can pursue your husband's interests. The differences between you can either divide or unite, partly depending upon how you respond to them.

4. What conscious choice will you make today to act in servant love toward your husband according to what the Lord has shown you this week? (Be specific.)

_____

_____

_____ ■

Will you make a move toward unity?

Will you lay down your own needs in order to lavish love on your man?

Will you commit to learning about how to experience and communicate your sexual pleasure?

God's desire for each of us as wives is that we choose servant love. May we grow to become servant lovers!

Pursuing Pure Pleasure

I just can't accept that God wants me to lose control sexually with my husband. It seems wrong and worldly. If I ever really let myself go, I think I would feel dirty.—Clacey

Sex is the place where Derek and I connect. We both like to try new things. But honestly, I struggle with guilt sometimes. I never know if what we are doing is okay with God.
—Annemarie

Perhaps you have had thoughts like Clacey and Annemarie. We have surveyed wives in several countries and guess what? Wives everywhere want to know, "What does God say is okay in the bedroom?"

What happens in marital intimacy is between you and your husband. While marriage is public, sex is private. If you are married, you wear a ring publicly to state that fact. If you are a woman, your name even identifies you as married: Mrs.

People watch your marriage, the way you talk to each other, the way you affectionately touch each other. They see the looks of love, of tenderness, or of disapproval. But no one sees your sexual intimacy. It is private. Only God sees your intimate touch, bliss-filled sighs and sounds of pleasure. Sex is a sacred exchange of love between only you and your husband.

Only within the sacred confines of your marital covenant do you express the most intimate and vulnerable part of yourself. What excites you, delights you, intoxicates you . . . only your husband knows. What turns him on, spins him around into ecstasy, is

CHAPTER SIX

THEME:

Pure Pleasure is found when a Christian couple discovers what is okay in the bedroom for them personally.

THEME VERSE:

". . . and where the Spirit of the Lord is, there is freedom."
(2 Corinthians 3:17)

your treasured secret. You alone know his sexual fantasies, his struggles, his needs, and he alone knows yours. What you two lovers do in private is known only to you.

The intimate boundaries of your sexual relationship are what make sex beautiful, vulnerable, and create a deep *yada* knowing. However, because sex is so private, you may have questions and nowhere to voice them. Is what you are doing in private okay with God? Does He smile at you or do you hope He isn't looking because you aren't really sure He is pleased?

For this reason, we want to spend this week asking, searching, and exploring the secret questions of your heart from God's perspective. In order to enjoy all that the Lord has given you and your husband in the gift of sex, you have to grasp God's design for pure pleasure.

In this chapter, we are going to answer four questions:

1. Why are there sexual boundaries in marriage?

2. What does God say no to?

3. What does God say yes to?

4. What if my husband and I can't agree?

As you begin this week's study, will you pray this prayer asking God to give you His wisdom?

Lord, what does pure pleasure look like for us? We want to revel in the joy of intoxicating pleasure but we also want it to be pure. Would You define "pure" for me and my husband? Maybe what is pure for us might be different for other Christian couples, but I need to know what it is specifically in our intimacy. I don't want guilt and questions to continue to plague our intimacy. Please show us how to be free to enjoy the pure pleasure You have given.

DAY 1

God's Boundaries Are for Your Good

During these weeks together, we have studied many aspects of God's opinion on sex. One aspect we haven't yet addressed is that God has given us guidelines and boundaries about how our sexuality is designed to be expressed, even within the sanctuary of marriage.

If you asked ten women what God thinks about sex, you'd probably hear words like restrictive, prudish, and old-fashioned. Things have changed quite a bit in the last several thousand years. How can God's teaching in an ancient book still apply to how we approach sexuality today?

Although Paul and Moses didn't have to address questions about Internet porn or sex toys, sexual temptation has always been an issue. The Bible records accounts of rape, sexual abuse, sodomy, incest, and prostitution. Many of Solomon's proverbs are about what to do with our sexual impulses.

Before we get into specific biblical teaching about what's okay in the bedroom, we want to address the question, "Why does God give us sexual guidelines in the first place?"

Satan loves to paint God as the cosmic killjoy. Just like he whispered to Eve in the garden, he wants you to believe that God is trying to keep people from pleasure. He whispers that Christians are missing out on all the fun. But God is a loving Father who has reasons for the moral boundaries He gives His children.

Reason 1: God wants to keep you from pain.

You can travel the world and you won't hear comments like these:

"I am so glad that I slept with all those men before I got married. Those sexual relationships really prepared me for marriage."

"I love the fact that porn is part of our marriage. It makes me feel so safe to know that my husband thinks of other women when he is being intimate with me!"

Of course you haven't heard such absurd statements. Sleeping around and porn represent pain and regret. God's boundaries are designed to keep us from pain. What appears to be restrictive actually brings freedom.

Sin can feel good for a short period of time. For example, having sex in the heat of the moment with someone outside of marriage can be physically pleasurable. However, that pleasure will eventually sour and turn into pain.

♥ 1. Read James 1:14–16. What do these verses say about the eventual pain of sin?

_____

_____

_____ ∎

♥ 2. How have God's boundaries protected you from pain in your past? How has violating those boundaries brought pain into your life?

_____

_____

_____ ∎

Reason 2: God wants you to experience pure pleasure.

God wants to do more than protect you from pain. He has come that you might have an abundant life (John 10:10)! He made you a sexual woman for your fulfillment and pleasure. His guidelines exist so that you can experience all the pleasure and intimacy that He has designed you to know.

Psalm 19 is all about how wonderful God's revelation is. David says that God's guidelines are "sweeter than honey" and "more precious than gold." Although the boundaries God gives may seem to take away fun and happiness at first glance, David learned that they are precious and bring joy to life. Read what he wrote as he meditated on God's instructions:

The instructions of the Lord are perfect,
   reviving the soul.
The decrees of the Lord are trustworthy,
   making wise the simple.
The commandments of the Lord are right,
   bringing joy to the heart.
The commands of the Lord are clear,
   giving insight for living.
Reverence for the Lord is pure,
   lasting forever.
The laws of the Lord are true;
   each one is fair.
They are more desirable than gold,
   even the finest gold.
They are sweeter than honey,
   even honey dripping from the comb.
They are a warning to your servant,
   a great reward for those who obey them.
How can I know all the sins lurking in my heart?
   Cleanse me from these hidden faults.
Keep your servant from deliberate sins!
   Don't let them control me.
Then I will be free of guilt
   and innocent of great sin.
May the words of my mouth
   and the meditation of my heart
be pleasing to you,
   O Lord, my rock and my redeemer.
Psalm 19:7–14 NLT

There is so much beauty, truth, and wisdom in Psalm 19. We encourage you to take the whole psalm into your heart and make it a part of you.

3. Meditate on Psalm 19:7–11. List everything said about the Word of God in these verses.

_____

_____

_____

_____ ■

♥ 4. How can all that God's Word promises encourage you as you seek to discover God's Pure Pleasure for you in your sexual intimacy?

_____

_____

_____ ■

♥ 5. Do you truly believe that _all_ of God's guidelines are for your good and ultimate pleasure? Why or why not?

_____

_____

_____ ■

♥ 6. Read Psalm 19:12–14. As you begin this study about Pure Pleasure in the bedroom, write a prayer to God asking Him to reveal any sin in your mind, heart, or actions.

_____

_____

_____

_____ ■

♥ 7. Using verse 14 as a guide, write a commitment to God, thanking Him that He will lead you to His personal truth for you and your husband.

_____

_____

_____

_____ ■

You've seen that God's Word promises to revive your soul, give you wisdom, bring joy to your heart, and give you insight for living. What promises! You are choosing to bring the most intimate aspect of your life under the wisdom of God. Your heavenly Father is delighted that you are seeking to honor Him in your sexuality!

DAY 2

What Does God Say No To?

You've seen in Psalm 19 that God's Word is your guide. God has clearly established sexual boundaries within marriage and these prohibitions must be honored for your own good. But outside of these guidelines, God gives *tremendous* sexual freedom! In order to understand what God allows in marriage, we must first look at the ten things to which He has firmly said no.

We asked Linda's husband, who is a theologian, to make a list of what God says no to. Here are Dr. Jody Dillow's conclusions:

1. FORNICATION: Fornication is immoral sex. It comes from the Greek word *porneia*, which means "unclean." This broad term includes sexual intercourse outside of marriage (1 Corinthians 7:2; 1 Thessalonians 4:3), sleeping with your stepmother (1 Corinthians 5:1), sex with a prostitute (1 Corinthians 6:15), and adultery (Matthew 5:32).

2. ADULTERY: Adultery, or sex with someone who is not your spouse, is a sin and was punishable in the Old Testament by death (Leviticus 20:10). In the New Testament, Jesus expanded adultery to mean not just physical acts but emotional acts in the mind and heart (Matthew 5:28).

3. HOMOSEXUALITY: The Bible is very clear that for a man to have sex with a man or a woman to have sex with a woman is detestable to God (Leviticus 18:22; 20:13; Romans 1:27; 1 Corinthians 6:9).

4. IMPURITY: There are several Greek words that are translated as "impurity." To become "impure" (Greek, *molyno*) can mean to lose one's virginity[1] or to become defiled, due to living out a secular and essentially pagan lifestyle (1 Corinthians 6:9; 2 Corinthians 7:1). The Greek word *rupos* often refers to moral uncleanness in general (Revelation 22:11).

5. ORGIES: For a married couple to become involved in sex orgies with different couples is an obvious violation of (1), (2), and (4).

6. PROSTITUTION: Prostitution, which is paying for sex, is morally wrong and condemned throughout Scripture (Leviticus 19:29; Deuteronomy 23:17; Proverbs 7:4–27).

7. LUSTFUL PASSIONS: First, let me tell you what this does not mean. Lustful passion does not refer to the powerful, God-given sexual desire for each other enjoyed by a married man and woman. Instead, it refers to an unrestrained, indiscriminate sexual desire for men or women other than the person's marriage partner (Mark 7:21–22; Ephesians 4:19).

8. SODOMY: In the Old Testament, sodomy refers to men lying with men.[2] The English word means male homosexual intercourse or intercourse with animals.[3] Unfortunately, some Christian teachers have erroneously equated sodomy with oral sex. This is not the way the term is used in the Bible. The sodomites in the Bible were male homosexuals,[4] or temple prostitutes (both male and female).[5]

9. OBSCENITY AND COARSE JOKES: In Ephesians 4:29, Paul says, "Do not let any unwholesome talk come out of your mouths." The Greek word is very descriptive and literally means rotten or decaying. In Ephesians 5:4 (NASB), the Bible warns us to avoid "silly talk" or, as it is called in the King James Version, "coarse jesting." We have all been around people who can see a sexual connotation in some innocent phrase and then begin to snicker or laugh. This is wrong. However, this does not rule out sexual humor in the privacy of marriage but rather inappropriate sexual comments in a public setting.

10. INCEST: Incest, or sex with family members or relatives, is specifically forbidden in Scripture (Leviticus 18:7–18; 20:11–21).

    These are the ten sexual things forbidden by God.

God's opinion about what's okay in the bedroom is not a guessing game. He wants us to have complete confidence that we can please Him with our actions and enjoy the pleasure of being sexually intimate with our husbands. So why do Christian wives go decades without the assurance of knowing what God thinks about certain sexual acts? Where does this confusion come from?

Apart from these things listed above, there is freedom. What does that mean? It means that there are no lists or rules about many of the things you and your husband want to do sexually together. It means that you have to figure out how to honor God with your freedom. It would be nice if God listed every possible sexual act in His Word with a yes or no by it.

Sex Toys: ☐ Yes ☐ No   **Oral Sex:** ☐ Yes ☐ No   **Self-Pleasuring:** ☐ Yes ☐ No

No such list exists! God wants you to seek Him, to talk and pray with your husband, to beg God for His wisdom.

♥ 1. Why do you think many women would rather have a list of dos and don'ts sexually instead of having to grapple with their freedom?

_____

_____

_____ ∎

♥ 2. How do you feel about not having dos and don'ts in the bedroom?

_____

_____

_____ ∎

The Bible is very clear that the freedom that God gives us sexually (and in other areas) is not a license to do whatever we want.

♥ 3. Look up 1 Peter 2:16 and write it in your own words below.

_____

_____

_____ ∎

Christians have struggled with how to use their freedom ever since they learned about it. In the early church, people asked questions about things like whether it was okay to eat meat that was sacrificed to idols and whether they should take part in observing pagan holidays. We don't have these same questions, but Paul's responses to the first Christians about their issues can help us figure out how God wants us to approach freedom in the bedroom.

♥ 4. Read 1 Corinthians 10:23–32. What principles do you see in these verses that teach you how to use the freedom God has given you? (We see at least five.)

_____

_____

_____ ∎

♥ 5. How might each of these principles apply to questions that Christian couples have in the bedroom?

_____

_____

_____ ∎

We hope that as you study God's Word, you have a clearer understanding of God's view on different expressions of sexuality. Through your study, you may have discovered that you (and perhaps your husband) are engaging in things God says no to. If so, confess those before the Lord and ask for His wisdom to pursue pure pleasure!

DAY 3

What Does God Say Yes To?

(Juli)

The other day, my nine-year-old son was invited to go over to a friend's house. As I dropped him off for his playdate, I said a few things to him: "I want you to have a great time. But remember to use your manners and be grateful." With these few instructions, I told my son that the purpose of the playdate was for him to have fun. My son has spent enough time under my parenting to know what I meant by "use your manners and be grateful." I didn't have to spell out to him exactly how to respond in the face of hundreds of potential scenarios like being served something he doesn't want to eat or being teased by his friend's little sister. The guidelines I gave were enough for him to use his judgment.

This example is similar to what you face in the bedroom. God's ultimate desire for your sexuality is for you to experience great pleasure and deep *yada* in your marriage. God says yes to a fulfilling, exciting sex life. He has given you and your husband some guidelines but also expects you to apply principles to the specifics of your marriage.

You have a list of the ten things God prohibits. You have also begun to study some principles on how to use your sexual freedom in the privacy of your one-flesh intimacy. But you need wisdom to know how to walk out all this in your own bedroom.

 1. Read 1 Corinthians 6:12 and paraphrase it here in your own words.

_____

_____

_____ ∎

Now look at this verse in other versions:

You say, "I am allowed to do anything"—but not everything is good for you. And even though "I am allowed to do anything," I must not become a slave to anything. (NLT)

Everything is permissible (allowable and lawful) for me; but not all things are helpful (good for me to do, expedient and profitable when considered with other things). Everything is lawful for me, but I will not become the slave of anything or be brought under its power. (AMP)

Just because something is technically legal doesn't mean that it's spiritually appropriate. If I went around doing whatever I thought I could get by with, I'd be a slave to my whims. (MSG)

"Everything is permissible for me"—but not everything is beneficial. (NIV)

Do you see the freedom God gives you to decide what is good, loving, and beneficial for you and your husband? You have amazing freedom! Many questions about sexual acts will be decided between you and your husband as a couple. God graciously gives *you* the freedom to determine your boundaries of what is loving and beneficial in your intimate oneness.

Now let's apply these verses to your personal questions about "What is okay for me and my husband?" You may wonder about things like:

"Is it okay to videotape my husband and me having sex just for our own viewing?"

"Is anal sex wrong?"

"My husband and I like to role-play during sex. Is this wrong?"

"I can only be stimulated by using a vibrator but I always feel guilty. Is this wrong?"

We want to give you three questions based on Scripture to ask about any sexual act you and your husband are considering. We believe this guide will help you discover God's wisdom for you.

DOES GOD SAY NO? Go to your list on pages 101–102 and ask the Lord to show you if the sexual act fits among prohibitions. If not, we may assume it is permitted. "Everything is permissible for me" (1 Corinthians 6:12).

IS IT GOOD FOR US? Does the practice in any way harm my husband or me or hinder our sexual relationship? Does it cause emotional or physical pain for one of us? Could it cause someone to stumble in their walk with the Lord? If so, it is not for you. "Everything is permissible for me—but not everything is beneficial" (1 Corinthians 6:12).

IS IT ONLY US? Hebrews 13:4 says, "Marriage should be honored by all, and the marriage bed kept pure . . ."

The marriage bed is to be kept pure. This means that it is never acceptable to involve someone else in sexual intimacy, including images, movies, fantasies, and even sexually explicit romance novels. The real or imagined presence of someone else will taint and compromise God's design for intimacy. So you do not bring someone else into your one-flesh intimacy in your mind, in your heart, on a DVD, on a computer screen, or on a piece of paper.

Okay, now it is your turn to apply these three questions!

💙 2. Suppose a close friend asks you this question: "My husband wants to videotape us making love—he thinks it would be a real turn-on for us to watch it together. Of course, no one else would ever watch it." How do you help her with her question?

FIRST ASK, *Does God say no?* (Consult the list on pages 101–102.)

Write what you discover here.

_____

_____

_____ ▪

SECOND ASK, *Is it good for us?* "Everything is permissible for me—but not everything is beneficial" (1 Corinthians 6:12).

Write your thoughts here.

_____

_____

_____ ■

THIRD ASK, *Is it only us?*

Write your thoughts here.

_____

_____

_____ ■

♥ 3. A second friend asks you, "Do you think it is wrong to use sex toys?"

FIRST ASK, *Does God say no?* (Consult the list on pages 101–102.)

Write what you discover here.

_____

_____

_____ ■

SECOND ASK, *Is it good for us?* "Everything is permissible for me—but not everything is beneficial" (1 Corinthians 6:12).

_____

_____

_____ ■

THIRD ASK, *Is it only us?*

Write your thoughts here.

_____

_____

_____ ■

We like the advice given by Dr. Lewis Smedes. "The Christian word on trying out a sexual practice that is not prohibited in Scripture is, 'Try it. If you like it, it is morally good for you. And it may well be that in providing new delight to each other, you will be adventuring into deeper experiences of love.'"[6]

God gives incredible freedom and He asks you to seek His wisdom. Sometimes a sexual act will seem beneficial in one situation but not in another. A great illustration of this is self-pleasuring. We often get asked questions about whether or not it is permissible for the husband or wife to engage in masturbation. The answer is different depending upon the situation.

Sara and Greg are worlds apart when it comes to their sexual relationship. Intimacy in their marriage has been marked by conflict, rejection, and pain. Over the years, they have learned that it is just easier to meet their own needs. Sara pleasures herself while reading a good romance novel that carries her away to a land in which she can imagine being loved and pursued. Greg has chosen to channel his sexual needs into regular masturbation.

Dana and Garrett have also experienced some frustration working through their differences in the bedroom. However, they are learning to communicate and be a team. Garrett is in the armed forces and has been deployed for several months at a time. Dana and Garrett recognize the temptation their absence creates for both of them, particularly for Garrett, who is often exposed to porn and opportunities to go places like strip clubs. Together, they have decided to self-pleasure while they are apart, thinking of intimate times they have had together.

4. These two couples are both engaging in the same act but for different reasons. Why might Sara and Greg be doing something that does not please God while Dana and Garrett are using their freedom appropriately?

_____

_____

_____ ∎

5. Given the example of these two couples, why is it so important to look beyond the actions to the intentions when using our freedom?

_____

_____

_____ ∎

There are a few more angles to consider when deciding if you and your husband are free to engage in a specific sexual act. As you found in I Corinthians 6:12, Paul says, "I am allowed to do anything, I must not become a slave to anything" (NLT). How does this apply to marital intimacy? Amy's situation might shed some light on it:

For the most part, I'm open to trying new things in our sexual relationship. But Stan is always pushing the envelope. At first it was new positions. Then it was having sex in new places. Lately, Stan has been bringing home sex toys and books on new things to try. What satisfied him last month doesn't work anymore. He cannot even get aroused without us doing something new and, in my opinion, kinky. Nothing he has suggested is immoral, per se, but I'd just like for us to be able to enjoy "normal sex" without always needing something new.

What Amy described in her marriage gives an example of how something she and her husband are free to do may be resulting in something that masters them or becomes addictive. While trying new things in the bedroom is fine, constantly needing to push the envelope is a concern.

Related to this is the question about sexual activity involving bondage and/or sadomasochism (BDSM). More women are asking us this question due to the use of it in "mommy porn" books. First, we want to be really clear about what these activities are and are not.

Perhaps your husband wants to tie your hands and blindfold you in order to heighten your sensations during sexual play. Maybe your lovemaking at times becomes intense and you rip the buttons off your husband's shirt in the heat of passion. We do not consider these examples to be BDSM but just healthy sex play between a husband and wife.

BDSM involves some measure of harm or humiliation for the purpose of sexual pleasure. Remember what God says yes to? Things that are loving and mutually beneficial. Inflicting pain or humiliation on your spouse, even if it is sexually arousing, is not loving and beneficial.

DAY 4

What If My Husband and I Can't Agree?

My husband has an adventurous spirit in our sexual relationship. He likes to have sex with me in lots of different places, like parked in a public parking lot, a locked restroom at a restaurant, in the woods, on the beach at night, and yes, we are members of the "mile high club." I usually give into these adventures. Fortunately, we have never been caught in the act, but I always feel uncomfortable. Should I keep going along with his adventurous requests?—Carrie

Your unique scenario may be different than Carrie's, but how do you respond when you and your husband disagree about what is okay for you to enjoy?

Step 1: Decide if it is an issue of comfort or conscience.

There is a big difference between violating your conscience ("I believe this is wrong") and pushing your comfort level ("I'm not sure I like this"). We stand firm on issues of conscience but need to be considerate when something is simply uncomfortable.

The principles of how we use our Christian freedom to glorify God and love each other apply not just to dictating what we don't do but also what we choose to do. There are some things that may not be comfortable or immediately pleasurable for you. But you may choose to do them because they are loving and sacrificial in meeting the needs of your husband. You are seeking to think not only of your own interests but of your husband and what will please him.

 1. You spent a lot of time last week studying Philippians 2:3–4. As a refresher, write them here. How do these verses apply when you and your husband don't agree on a sexual practice?

_____

_____

_____

_____

_____

_____

_____

_____

_____

GETTING PERSONAL WITH *Linda*

Here's a story about me pushing past my comfort zone. I remember like it was yesterday . . . during the first year of marriage, Jody said to me, "Honey, I want you to tell me in detail everything you're going to do to pleasure me and I want you to tell me in detail everything you want me to do to pleasure you." I said, "In detail." I was embarrassed, I didn't want to do what he'd asked. What words would I use? How could I say such things out loud? I remember thinking, *Okay, Linda, you can claim embarrassment and say, "I just can't do that," or you can swallow your embarrassment and delight your husband by doing what he asked.* And yes, it was hard the first time and I'm sure I blushed but the second time it was easier. Now I smile gratefully that I jumped over that first hurdle and many others to become the lover of my husband's dreams.

♥ 2. Read I Corinthians 13:4–8a. How does this beautiful passage on unconditional love apply when you and your husband don't agree about a sexual act?

_____

_____

_____ ■

Violating your conscience involves more than just pushing past your comfort level. It is the conviction that something is morally wrong.

♥ 3. What does I Corinthians 10:23–32 say about how your conscience is involved in using Christian freedom?

_____

_____

_____ ■

♥ 4. Write a paragraph describing the difference between violating your conscience in the bedroom and pushing against your comfort?

_____

_____

_____ ■

Step 2: Communicate your feelings to your husband.

Disagreements about what to do in the bedroom become more explosive because most couples don't know how to communicate how they are feeling. Has this ever happened to you?

In the midst of making love, your husband says, does, or suggests something that you don't want to do. You're not sure how to respond, so you just freeze. Perhaps in frustration you just say, "Stop it! I don't want to do that." The passion cools immediately and the topic never surfaces again until the next time he makes the same move.

As uncomfortable as it may be, you and your husband can never understand and honor each other sexually unless you communicate about why you want or don't want to do something. These conversations need to happen during times of intimacy but not during sexual intimacy!

Because finding the right words can be difficult, here is a suggestion of what to say or write to your husband when you just can't agree.

Babe, first I just want you to know that I'm all for our intimacy and I want to grow to become more of the lover you want and need. Our intimacy is special to me. I need to tell you, though, that this sexual act (name it)_____that we've been arguing about is just something I can't do. (Clarify if it is because you believe it is on the list of "What's Not Okay" or if you're just uncomfortable with it.) Can we talk together about something new and exciting that we can both agree on? Because I really want to please you.

Step 3: Make a decision together based on what is loving.

Kendra had suffered years of sexual abuse from an uncle as a child. The abuse always involved oral sex. When she married Tom, a wonderful man, she could not bring herself to engage in oral sex. Just the thought of a penis in her mouth brought up immediate feelings of shame and revulsion. Tom felt rejected every time he asked for it and Kendra refused. Eventually, Kendra was able to communicate to Tom how oral sex brought back terrible memories and sensations.

For Kendra, engaging in oral sex with her husband wasn't just about pushing past what she felt comfortable with. It brought back the trauma from her past and made her feel unsafe in their intimacy. Although this couple was free to enjoy this sexual act, it would not be loving for Tom to insist on it.

Once Tom understood his wife's past, he lovingly said to her, "I will never ask you to do something that causes you pain like this. We will find other ways of enjoying each other."

♥ 5. Read 1 Corinthians 10:24 and write it here. How can this verse be a guide to you and your husband when you disagree about sexual questions?

_____

_____

_____

_____ ■

♥ 6. If you have been wrestling with some "Is it okay?" questions about sexuality in your marriage, how can you use what you have learned to experience the freedom God has given you and your husband?

_____

_____

_____ ■

DAY 5

The Secret Place: Wisdom

Throughout decades of ministry, we have ministered to many, many women in the areas of marriage and sexual intimacy. Between the two of us, we've been asked about every question imaginable. Our conclusion is this: You need God's wisdom and He is willing to give it to you!

Friend, your marriage is unique. There is no other couple in the world who has the exact same needs, struggles, history, personality, and questions as you and your man. The principles you studied this week are the starting place of wisdom. But you also need God's help to apply those principles to your own unique journey toward pure pleasure.

Your God is a God of wisdom. The Hebrew word for wisdom in the Old Testament is *hokmah*. It means "the use of knowledge in a practical and successful way."[7] This interesting Hebrew word speaks of having skill. It is the word used in Exodus 35 about the women who created beautiful fabrics and tapestries for the tabernacle.

Every skilled woman spun with her hands . . . and all the women who were willing and had the skill spun the goat hair. (Exodus 35:25–26)

When we look at the meaning of the Hebrew word for wisdom, an accurate rendering of wisdom would be:

Wisdom is taking the knowledge you have about God and applying it in a skillful way so you live life as a thing of beauty.

This applies in your marriage: Respecting your husband is applying God's wisdom in a skillful way so your marriage will become a thing of beauty.

This applies in your sexual intimacy: This week God has given you wisdom about His boundaries and His freedom in the bedroom. He desires you to take this knowledge and apply it in a skillful way so your lovemaking will be a thing of beauty.

For the Lord gives wisdom, and from his mouth come knowledge and understanding . . . you will understand what is right and just and fair—every good path. For wisdom will enter your heart, and knowledge will be pleasant to your soul. (Proverbs 2:6, 9–10)

💙 1. Write a paragraph describing how these verses from Proverbs apply to your intimate relationship with your husband.

_____

_____

_____

_____

_____

_____

_____ ■

Wisdom also has a moral quality. It is certainly possible to be skillful and immoral. Ability without morality is foolishness.

♥ 2. Read Proverbs 1:7 and Psalm 36:1–4. What do these verses teach you about the wisdom of following God's guidelines?

_____

_____

_____ ■

Wisdom is essential to you as you strive for pure pleasure in your marriage! You need God's help to know how to respond in those tense moments, when to say yes, and how to say no. The great news is that God's wisdom is readily available to you. Do you know how pleased your heavenly Father is that you would cry out to Him for wisdom?

♥ 3. Read James 1:5 and paraphrase it here applying it to your sexual intimacy.

_____

_____

_____ ■

♥ 4. If there is a special area you need wisdom for, fall to your knees, pour out your heart, knowing that God is the only One who knows the way you should go. Read Psalm 139:23–24.

_____

_____

_____

_____

_____

_____

_____

_____ ■

5. Take ten or fifteen minutes and read back through this week's lesson, thanking God for everything you have learned. Thank Him for your new understanding of what is prohibited and what is permitted in your intimacy. Thank Him that He longs to give you wisdom for every question in your heart. Write a prayer of thanksgiving to God here or in your journal.

_____

_____

_____

_____

_____

_____

_____

_____

_____

_____ ■

And as you write your prayer of thanksgiving to God, we would like to pray over you.

Creative Creator God, thank You that You promise to give Your daughter skill in living life—You call this wisdom. Lord God, she needs Your wisdom in every area of her life. Today, we ask that You will show her how to take the knowledge she has about sexual intimacy, the understanding of what You approve, and what You don't approve, and teach her how to skillfully love her husband. May she live under the protection of Your holiness in this private area of sexual intimacy so it can become a thing of beauty.

Exposing Counterfeit Intimacy

CHAPTER SEVEN

THEME:

Both temptation and God's strength to stand against it are guarantees.

THEME VERSE:

"No temptation has seized you except what is common to man. And God is faithful; he will not let you be tempted beyond what you can bear. But when you are tempted, he will also provide a way out so that you can stand up under it." (1 Corinthians 10:13)

Let us introduce you to Kathy, a very committed Christian woman who had a dilemma. She and Rob had been married for twenty-one years of fading passion and no common interests. Within the last year, Kathy met Keith, the man of her dreams. They shared a love for God, for ministry, and for life. As they talked about these things, they discovered a strong attraction that contrasted with each of their lifeless marriages.

> I believe God brought Keith into my life because He knows how lonely and miserable I am with Rob. Keith and I pray and read the Bible together. On one level, I know this affair is wrong but also believe that it's from God. He wants us to be together! I've never felt so happy and fulfilled. We can serve God more effectively together than apart.

If your head is spinning by the contradictions of Kathy's thinking, you are not alone. How could these Christ followers be reading the Bible, praying, and serving together while also having an adulterous affair?

Did Kathy and Keith just skip over certain passages of the Bible?

Did they shove their wedding vows in a "Do not remember" hiding place?

Did they forget about the respect of their children?

How had they convinced themselves that God was part of their sin? What happened to Kathy and

Keith can very easily and quickly happen to you and me. Maybe you're saying, "No way, that couldn't happen to me. I just wouldn't be that deceived."

No one sets out to fall into temptation and deception. However, every man and woman will someday, somehow experience the powerful temptation to be unfaithful emotionally or sexually in his or her marriage. If you think it could never happen to you, consider a warning from Oswald Chambers: "An unguarded strength is a double weakness."[1] Jesus warned you that the flesh is very weak:

> Keep watching and praying that you may not enter into temptation; the spirit is
> willing, but the flesh is weak. (Matthew 26:41 NASB)

Every sexual temptation is rooted in the deep longings of your heart to be loved and known. You were created for a deep *yada* knowing! God has provided for each of us to experience *yada* through unity and intimacy with God through Jesus Christ and the fellowship of His Holy Spirit. And yes, we can also experience the deep *yada* knowing through sexual expression in marriage.

Satan takes the holy desire for *yada* and presents us with shortcuts—counterfeits that appear to meet the longings of our heart but end in hurt, rejection, and shame. Every one of us, married or single, is vulnerable to counterfeit intimacy. Emotional affairs, fantasies about the "perfect man" sweeping us off our feet, sexual chat rooms, and pornography are just a few of the ways that men and women fall into the traps of counterfeit intimacy.

This week's theme verse reminds you of three things you must keep in mind as you look at the temptations of counterfeit intimacy:

1. To be tempted is part of the normal, human condition. Jesus was tempted.
Be prepared because you will be, too.

2. God is faithful to provide you the strength to stand and a way of escape
when tempted.

3. God will provide the strength to stand and a way of escape, *but you must choose it.*

DAY 1

The Anatomy of Temptation

A few years ago, a high profile football team was caught cheating. The New England Patriots were filming the defensive signals of their opponents so that they knew the enemy's game plan before the plays even started. If their opponent planned to defend against a running play, the Patriots took advantage by passing the ball. By knowing their enemy's strategy, they could win the game.

What the Patriots did was unethical because sports teams are not supposed to have an unfair advantage. However, the same rules do not apply to standing against our enemy. We are not playing a game. We are in a war.

God has given us a peek at the enemy's playbook. In God's Word, we have many stories and passages that tell us how our enemy will try to entice us to sin. Today, we want to look at one passage in particular that lays out precisely how we fall into temptation.

> And remember, when you are being tempted, do not say, "God is tempting me." God is never tempted to do wrong, and he never tempts anyone else. Temptation comes from our own desires, which entice us and drag us away. These desires give birth to sinful actions. And when sin is allowed to grow, it gives birth to death. (James 1:13–15 NLT)

♥ 1. James 1:13–15 is an important passage. We encourage you to memorize it! You can use your favorite version of the Bible or the New Living Translation quoted above. Plant these two verses in your mind! Make them a part of you. Paraphrase them here.

_____

_____

_____ ∎

In these verses we see the downward spiral of temptation. So let's take the passage apart and see the steps of progression.

Step 1: Temptation
Step 2: Contemplation
Step 3: Activation
Step 4: Death

The first step is Temptation, stemming from your desires

James says that the first step in temptation begins with the **evil desires** we have in our hearts. Temptation doesn't start with God or even with Satan but with our *own* heart.

What evil desires could possibly lead to sexual temptation? Here are a few to consider:

Pride: "I deserve better than this marriage."

Covetousness: "I wish my husband treated me like that."

Lust: "It's not a big deal to let my mind go there. I'm not acting on it."

Bitterness: "Why should I meet his needs? When is the last time he did something for me?"

Sometimes temptation begins with the desire to find a "shortcut" to experience sexual pleasure or deep connection.

What would you do if you were running a 10K race, you felt exhausted, and you saw a secret path that would eliminate a significant part of the course without anyone knowing it? Would you be tempted to take the shortcut?

There are many shortcuts to sexual pleasure or feelings of "love." Instead of investing the mental and physical energy into pursuing true passion, you might pull up a steamy scene from a movie or romance novel. You might think of someone other than your husband. Here's how a few women described their frustration with "shortcuts."

"I hate it, just hate it. I'll be making love with my husband and this image from my before-Christ days floods into my mind. It is erotic, it excites me, and I don't want that old image to excite me. I want to be totally present and excited about my husband."

"I just can't conjure up romantic, erotic feelings about my husband. He has gained a lot of weight and just isn't sexy to me. It's much easier for me to fantasize about making love to a stranger. I can get excited almost immediately."

The second step of temptation is Contemplation. "We are dragged away and enticed based on evil desire" (James 1:14).

What began as a seed in your heart of wanting or wishing for something more, all of a sudden has become a hook for the enemy. The words "dragged away" and "enticed" suggest an outside force taking advantage of our internal weaknesses.

♥ 2. Have you ever experienced the enemy "dragging you away" or "enticing" you? How did it happen?

_____

_____

_____

♥ 3. Read Genesis 39. This is a case study of sexual temptation.

a. Who did Joseph say sexual sin was against?

_____

_____

b. How often did this temptation come at Joseph?

_____

_____

c. Joseph said no to the temptation but he was still put in jail. Do you think this was fair?

_____

_____

d. What was God's response to Joseph desiring to do right?

_____

_____ ■

Notice that Joseph did not sin! To have evil desires is normal. For the enemy to try to exploit those desires is also part of the Christian life. It is not a sin to be tempted. It is at this point that you and every other person faces a fork in the road. Do you step into sin or do you stand against it?

The third step of temptation is Activation. "Desire is conceived (or nurtured) and it gives birth to sin" (James 1:15).

The activation of temptation is when we *choose* to step into sin with our lingering thoughts and actions. There is a very fine and definite line from being tempted by our desire and choosing to step into sin. Temptation is nurtured and gains strength in darkness and secrecy. It gains footing when we tell ourselves it's no big deal—that we can handle one more look or a little flirtation.

Talia worked for a Christian ministry and began a friendship with a male coworker. As she and this guy, Scott, got to know each other, their relationship became more casual and playful. One day, Talia noticed that she was more conscious of what she chose to wear if Scott was going to be in a meeting. She also noticed that her heart skipped a beat when an email from him popped up in her in-box. Talia was at the crossroads of temptation. The Lord was showing her that this relationship was dangerous. As a married woman she was perilously close to a terrible choice.

♥ 4. What would it look like for Talia, at this point, to nurture desire and step into sin?

_____

_____

_____ ■

The final step of temptation is Death. "And when sin is allowed to grow, it gives birth to death" (James 1:15 NLT).

The crossroads of temptation is not just a choice between sin and righteousness. It is also a choice between life and death. Proverbs 7 is written to men about the dangers of sexual temptation; the truth of its message applies to our temptations too.

♥ 5. What does Proverbs 7:21–27 say about the end result of sexual sin?

_____

_____

_____ ■

Sexual sin ends in death. Obviously, this is not a physical death or there would be a lot of dead husbands and wives lying around! It is the death of a marriage, the death of the respect of your children. The death of your respect for you and for choices.

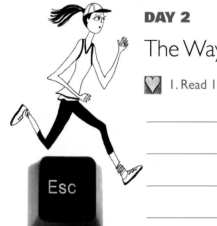 6. Ask the Lord this week to open your eyes to the vulnerabilities in your heart and your marriage to the temptations of counterfeit intimacy. Write a prayer asking Him to teach you to stand and choose life.

_____

_____

_____ ∎

DAY 2

The Way of Escape

1. Read 1 Corinthians 10:13 and paraphrase it here.

_____

_____

_____

_____

_____ ∎

Maybe your husband has made a small or a *big* error sexually. You know he is tempted . . . he is a man. But what about you? I, Linda, was involved in surveying three hundred Christian women. They were asked, "Have you ever been tempted by another man?" Ninety-five percent of them said yes and I wondered if the other 5 percent were either newlyweds or lying! If you're thinking, *this will never happen to me*, think again. Chances are that sometime during your marriage, it will happen to you. So are you prepared? Are you in battle mentality?

Your battle plan begins today! If you wait until the temptation has a face and name, you won't fare well. There are some important choices you need to make now. They will involve four strategic steps.

1. Make a list of your "I wills."
2. Tell a friend.
3. Flee!
4. Keep watching and keep praying!

♥ 2. Read Psalm 25:20–21 and write it here.

_____

_____

_____

_____

_____

_____

_____

_____

_____

_____ ▪

♥ 3. Do you have a strategy to guard your soul and let integrity and uprightness preserve you? If so, write a paragraph describing it.

_____

_____

_____

_____

_____

_____

_____

_____

_____

_____ ▪

GETTING PERSONAL WITH *Linda*

Let me share with you what I have done. Psalm 101 is the psalmist David's list of "I wills." He sets out who he desires to be in public and in private. David's psalm of commitment has encouraged and motivated me to have a private list of my "I wills." These are secret choices I have made before the Lord about how I long to live based on Psalm 101.

I will sing of your love and justice.
I will praise you with songs.
I will be careful to live a blameless life.
I will lead a life of integrity in my own home.
I will refuse to look at anything vile and vulgar.
I will have nothing to do with those who deal crookedly.
I will reject perverse ideas and stay away from every evil.
I will not tolerate people who slander their neighbors.
I will not endure conceit and pride.
I will search for faithful people to be my companions.
I will not allow deceivers to serve in my house.

First step: Have a list of your "I wills."

💜 4. Using Psalm 101 as a guide, write a list of your "I wills." This is your battle plan to fight temptation.

_____

_____

_____

_____

_____

_____

_____

_____ ■

Maggie, a young wife, made a list of her "I wills":

I **WILL** walk with integrity in my home.
I **WILL** not entertain thoughts of another man in my mind.
I **WILL** not entertain thoughts of another man in my heart.
I **WILL** not entertain thoughts of another man in my body.
I **WILL** seek friends who also choose to be faithful as my companions.

David's declaration in Psalm 101 is beautiful, and we're sure he meant every word when he wrote it. But David didn't lead a life of integrity in his own home. He fell to temptation. David needed an escape route when he was tempted with evil. So what is your escape route when you are tempted in your mind, heart, or body?

Second step: Tell a friend.

As long as something remains hidden, it has power, but when we bring the secret out into the open, its power is broken. Tell a mentor or friend and bring it into the light. Don't wait, tell a friend _today_!

💜 5. Write the name of the friend or mentor you will tell here. If you don't have a trusted woman friend, ask God to give you one.

_____

_____

_____ ■

Third step: Flee!

 6. Read 1 Corinthians 6:18 and write it here. The word *flee* is a strong command. Write a paragraph describing what it would look like for you to run fast from sexual sin?

_____

_____

_____

_____

_____

_____

_____

_____

_____

_____ ∎

This command means to cut off sin today:

If you are entertaining thoughts of another man, cut it off today!

If you are involved emotionally with another man, cut it off today!

If you are involved sexually with another man, cut it off today!

And all these ways of fleeing and cutting off sin also apply if you are involved not with a man but with a woman.

Fourth step: Keep watching and keep praying!

"Keep watching and praying that you may not enter into temptation; the spirit is willing, but the flesh is weak" (Matthew 26:41 NASB).

These are Jesus' words urging us to not just watch for a day or pray every now and then but keep on watching and keep on praying. Why? Because He says our spirits long to do right but our flesh is just plain weak.

GETTING PERSONAL WITH Juli

Watching and praying sounds pretty spiritual. Making it practical is a little more difficult. This is why "The Secret Place" has become so important to me. When I have quiet time on my knees with the Lord, I ask Him to search my heart. Often He reveals thought patterns and temptations that I would simply skip past in the busyness of life. To me, watching and praying means being diligent to tend the garden of my heart. I don't want to look past small weeds just because they are small. I want the Lord to show me where my heart is vulnerable to sin so that I can turn from it before it has a chance to grow.

♥ 7. Write a prayer to God expressing how you will keep watching and keep praying.

_____

_____

_____

_____

_____

_____ ∎

DAY 3

Dealing with Your Husband's Temptations

The most traumatic day in Sabrina's life was discovering her husband's involvement in pornography. Sabrina knew that Andrew had struggled with porn before they were married, but she assumed it wasn't an issue anymore since he had a regular sexual outlet. She never thought twice about their unfiltered computer or the sexually explicit material available on their satellite network. One night, Sabrina woke up to find that Andrew wasn't in bed. She moseyed into the home office, expecting to find her husband at work. Instead, she saw him masturbating to erotic images on the computer screen. Sabrina was sick and horrified. A contrite and humiliated Andrew attempted to calm his wife and assured her that this was an isolated incident.

Sabrina felt so rejected and defiled that she couldn't stand Andrew's touch. He tried to console her, but she didn't want to even be near him. What did this mean for their marriage? Wasn't she enough to satisfy him? What else was he into?

If your husband has been involved in an affair with another woman or in pornography, you know the trauma of what Sabrina experienced. You question everything: his love for you, your desirability, his credibility. Every sexual experience you've ever had with your husband is now viewed through a different lens.

We want to walk you through some biblical and practical principles to help you understand and address your husband's unique sexual temptations. We recognize that for some of you, this is a very sensitive and painful topic. Our desire is to point you to God's Word and wisdom, whatever situation you and your husband may be confronting. There are two key attitudes God calls for your heart and mind to embrace.

1. Have empathy for the struggle.

2. Do not enable the sin.

In our work helping women walk through a husband's temptation, we have seen very few approach their husband's struggles and failings with both empathy and a call to accountability. Yet, every time Scripture calls for one Christian to deal with another's sin, both of these elements are taught.[2]

First key: Growing in empathy

♥ 1. What do you think it means to have empathy in the midst of your husband's sexual temptations and failings?

_____

_____

_____ ∎

The dictionary defines *empathy* this way:

"The action of understanding, being aware of, being sensitive to, and vicariously experiencing the feelings, thoughts, and experience of another . . ."

Empathy means that you understand what it is like to be your husband. The problem is that you have never been a man and cannot fully grasp what it is like to be tempted as he is. You can't get your mind around why your husband might be completely captivated and mesmerized by a glimpse of a woman in a string bikini. You can't imagine the fact that some days he fights moment by moment not to think about sexual things.

Although you cannot understand your husband's temptations, you know what it feels like to battle against sin. Empathy begins with humility, the acknowledgment that you are just as flawed and broken as your husband is. If you are honest, you struggle with sin just like he does, but your sin may be less obvious. It could be anxiety, self-righteousness, the desire to be esteemed by others, gossip, bitterness, complaining, dishonesty, wishing you had a different husband.

♥ 2. What sin pattern do you battle daily?

_____

_____

_____ ∎

♥ 3. Each of the following passages teaches how we are to think about and address someone else's sin. In what way does each of these passages encourage you to have a heart of understanding and empathy toward your husband in this situation?

a. Matthew 7:1–5

_____

_____

_____ ∎

b. John 8:1–11

_____

_____

_____ ∎

c. Galatians 6:1–4

_____

_____

_____ ∎

Empathy also means understanding that good men are tempted by sexual sin. For the average man, sexual temptation is a major aspect of his existence. The title of the bestselling book *Every Man's Battle* says it all. This book has sold over 2.5 million copies, affirming the fact that sexual temptation really is every man's battle.

Christian men who struggle with sexual temptation carry an enormous amount of shame. Just the fact that they are tempted to look at porn or think sexually about a coworker brings about thoughts like:

"What's wrong with me? No matter how hard I try, I can't stop thinking this way!"

"I hate myself for the thoughts I have. If anyone knew what really went through my mind, they would be disgusted."

We have met with wonderful, Christian men who doubt their salvation because the fight against lust was so great. A godly husband is *not* a man who doesn't struggle with sexual sin but one who continually fights and refuses to give in to temptation. We  saw earlier in this chapter that King David, one of the godliest men who ever walked the earth, not only experienced sexual temptation, he fell into it hook, line, and sinker!

♥ 4. To what extent do you believe you understand how your husband is tempted sexually? What fears keep you from wanting to know his struggles?

_____

_____

_____ ■

Second key: Empathy does not mean excusing sin.

While some wives have a difficult time understanding why their husbands struggle sexually, others approach the issue as if it is not a big deal. This is particularly true with porn. Sitcoms show couples joking about a husband using porn with his wife's full knowledge and consent as if it's just a normal part of marriage. We've heard wives buy into this thinking with statements like, "It's not like he's having an affair," or "It takes pressure off of me having to always satisfy him."

While Jesus extends overwhelming grace and forgiveness to us in our sin, He also calls us to a standard of holiness. As a godly wife, you are called to help your husband set his eyes on a standard of holiness in your marriage. But how do you do this?

One of the primary ways you can help your husband is to link his behavior with the impact on your marriage. Satan deceives men into compartmentalizing their sexual behavior. In other words, a man may believe that he can fantasize about another woman, flirt with someone at work, or look at sexual pictures on the Internet and that this has no impact on how deeply he loves his wife.

Sexual sin of any kind destroys the possibility of deep _yada_ knowing between you and your husband. You can help him make this link.

♥ 5. What impact does your husband's sexual sin or temptation have on you? On your marriage?

_____

_____

_____

_____ ■

Communicating the link of your husband's behavior to how you feel is a very delicate matter. Your husband may not be able to hear how his behavior affects you until he gets past the feelings of shame that fuel defensiveness. Your first step is to make sure that he feels validated in the struggle. This may take time. But eventually, he will be ready to hear and understand the link. Here is a sample script to help you communicate this concept.

I want you to know how deeply I desire to share all of life with you. I want to share our thoughts, our dreams, and our bodies completely. I understand that you struggle with _____ and I want to help you in whatever way I can to win that battle. But I also need you to understand how your struggle hurts me. It makes me feel like I'm worthless and like I can never please you (insert your own words). It chips away at the trust I so desperately want to have between us. I long for all of your sexual thoughts to only be about me. Please forgive me for how I have resisted you sexually. I want to work on becoming the kind of lover who captivates you. However, I can only give myself to you if I know that you are reserving all of who you are—body, soul, and mind—for me.

♥ 6. Read Matthew 18:15–35. Here Jesus tells us how to confront sin in each other and also teaches what our heart attitude should be. What specific instructions do you see in this teaching?

_____

_____

_____ ■

Walking this out practically means understanding the difference between a husband who is actively fighting temptation and one who will not admit his need for help.

♥ 7. Read 1 John 1:6–10. What does this passage say about the importance of heart attitude toward our sin struggles?

_____

_____

_____ ■

If your husband is open about his struggle, asking for forgiveness, and wanting help, do all you can to support him. If however, he denies that it is a problem and refuses to address it, you must begin lovingly drawing boundaries and creating an atmosphere that does not enable sin to continue. These decisions require great discernment, which is why Jesus tells us to bring in a wise third party (pastor or counselor) to help us walk biblically.

♥ 8. To close today's lesson, we would like to lead you into prayer concerning your husband's temptations.

Dear Lord,
You tell me to first take the plank out of my own eye before I even begin to understand and confront my husband's sin. In this moment, would You begin to show me my own sin, sexual or otherwise?

I confess before You my sins of _____ .

I admit that I am afraid to truly understand my husband's sexuality and how he struggles. It feels like too much for me to handle. Yet, I want to understand this man You have given me so that I can be his teammate in every way. Please give me the wisdom and empathy to walk beside him, embracing all of who he is.

Lord, give me the grace to always remember that I am a sinner and struggle just as he does. His sin is no more heinous than mine. Give me the words this week to know how to reach toward him in his struggle and become the helper that You designed me to be.

Amen

DAY 4

Fighting the Battle like a Team

One of the most damaging aspects of sexual temptation is that it divides couples. Very rarely do a husband or wife even discuss how they are tempted sexually unless one of them catches the other in the act: sending flirtatious texts to a coworker, watching something sexually explicit, reconnecting with an old flame on Facebook, or lying about why you were late coming home from the office.

Because of the shame and feelings of rejection associated with sexual temptations, most people keep it a secret from their spouse.

As much as Satan would love to have one or both of you fall into sexual sin, he is happy to use the temptation itself as a wedge between you. The last thing he wants is for you and your husband to work together in combating temptation!

Remember who the true enemy is. Regardless of which of you struggles with sexual temptation, you must begin to see this as your problem as a couple. We do not mean that a wife should take responsibility for her husband's purity or vice versa. However, when sexual sin and temptation hits one of you, it affects both of you. Satan will use pornography, inappropriate emotional attachments, and other forms of temptation to further divide you if he can define your spouse as "the problem" or "the enemy." As long as you are fighting each other, you cannot stand together.

Marriage is the ultimate team sport, so how do we become a team?

Becoming a team in combatting sexual temptation requires three things:

First, you must learn to communicate to each other without judgment. If you don't know how your husband struggles, how can you help him? If he doesn't know your struggles, how can he help you?

♥ 1. On a scale from 1 to 10, how well do you and your husband understand each other's vulnerabilities and temptations? How can you take a step to improve in this area?

_____

_____

_____ ▪

Second, you play defense together. Where is your marriage vulnerable? What needs do you and your husband have that are not being met, leaving you open to temptation? How can you put up "walls" or "hedges" to protect against temptation?

Wendy and Mark built hedges:

We won't have a meal alone with someone of the opposite sex.
We will try always to be available to take a phone call from our mate.
We'll keep all texts, voice mails, and email accounts available to each other.

♥ 2. What do you and your husband do to play defense together?

_____

_____

_____ ▪

Third, you play offense together. Don't just wait for temptation to attack your marriage. Pray against it. Work on your sexual and romantic relationship so that you do not leave room for the enemy to attack.

♥ 3. How do you and your husband play offense, guarding against possible temptation in your marriage?

_____

_____

_____ ▪

♥ 4. Read 1 Corinthians 7:1–5. Put it in your own words here:

_____

_____

_____ ▪

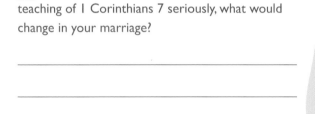 5. According to this passage, how specifically can you and your husband keep each other from sexual temptation?

_____

_____

_____ ∎

As you mediate on 1 Corinthians 7, we want to be very clear. You can be the most beautiful, faithful wife and still have a husband who makes sinful choices. We have met with women who were very eager to be an exciting lover and were married to men who fell into sexual sin. However, there are also many women who do not take Paul's teaching in 1 Corinthians 7 seriously. An important part of your ministry to your husband is embracing his sexuality and gifting him with yours. You are designed to be a major line of defense between your husband and sexual sin.

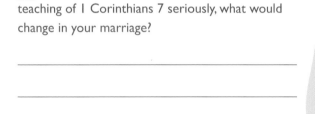 6. If you and your husband were to take the teaching of 1 Corinthians 7 seriously, what would change in your marriage?

_____

_____

_____

_____

_____ ∎

GETTING PERSONAL WITH *Juli*

Mike and I have learned over the years what it means to fight temptation as a team. At first, it seemed like an invasion of privacy to ask each other about how we were tempted. Then we realized that it was actually a step toward deep intimacy to be so vulnerable with each other. I must admit that playing "offense" is more fun than just playing "defense." But fighting together against the enemy has deepened our trust in each other and profoundly impacted our intimacy.

Ecclesiastes 4:12 can easily be applied to marriage:

Though one may be overpowered, two can defend themselves. A cord of three strands is not quickly broken.

This verse speaks of a cord of three strands. Remember that the Christian marriage is not made up of two but of three. You and your spouse do not stand against the enemy by yourselves. You stand with the person of the Lord Jesus Christ ready and able to fight with and for you. The Lord's opinion of your marriage is not neutral. He says in Hebrews 13:4 that the marriage bed should be pure and marriage should be honored by all. The

Practical questions about being a team.

As you and your husband work toward becoming a team in combating sexual temptation, there are two guidelines you need to understand:

1. Being a team doesn't mean being each other's primary accountability partners. Although it is healthy for a husband and wife to understand how and when the other is most tempted, we do not suggest that you trust only each other for accountability. You need a woman you trust to ask you the difficult questions and he needs another man to do the same for him.

2. Being a team doesn't mean you share every detail with each other. One of the reasons it is unwise to be your husband's accountability partner is that some details about how he is tempted (or how you are tempted) could be emotionally damaging and even traumatic. When a vivid picture of sexual temptation and/or failure is painted, those images are difficult to erase and can erode trust.

Almighty One also declares that whom He has joined together, let no one tear apart. Begin fighting the true enemy of your marriage as a team by reminding one another that, "If God is for us, who can be against us" (Romans 8:31)!

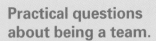 7. Now is the time to put some of what you have been learning into practice. Keeping all that you have studied this week in your own mind and heart will only go so far in combating sexual temptation. You and your husband must take steps toward becoming a team. We understand that each marriage is in a different place. You and your husband may have conversations about temptation regularly. Or this may be a topic you have never even considered broaching. Please choose the action assignment below that you believe is most appropriate for where you are in your marriage:

a. Read all or portions of this week's homework with your husband. Then ask each other the question, how can I better understand how you struggle sexually?

b. Ask your husband to commit to praying together with you once a week specifically about guarding your marriage against sexual temptation.

c. Write a letter to the Lord expressing fears and emotions that get in the way of you wanting to know and understand your husband's sexual temptations. Ask Him for wisdom and courage.

_____

_____

_____

_____

_____

_____

_____

DAY 5

The Secret Place: "I Will Remember"

Perhaps this lesson has stirred up grief in your heart. You remember your sexual sin or your husband's. Or maybe the temptation is not in the past but in the present and the grief is overwhelming. Wherever you are today in your marriage—delighting over the sweetness or agonizing over the pain—Psalm 77 will encourage your heart.

Psalm 77 is one of our favorites. We love it because Asaph, the author and one of King David's chief musicians, understood the depths of piercing pain. We rejoice in his honest description of grief and delight that he discovered a way to move from a sob of sorrow to a song of praise.

1. Read Psalm 77:1–10 and paraphrase it here.

_____

_____

_____

_____

_____ ∎

The New American Standard Bible translates verse 10 this way: "It is my grief that the right hand of the Most High has changed." Asaph was in such despair that he felt God had changed (verse 10). Life seemed hopeless.

2. Describe a time (perhaps it has been during this Bible study) when you experienced this deep, heart-wrenching agony.

_____

_____

_____ ∎

3. Read Psalm 77:11–14 and describe the shift in perspective.

_____

_____

_____ ∎

Something dramatic happens in Asaph's heart in the second half of Psalm 77. What brought about this amazing transformation? Three little words reveal what he did:

I will remember

 4. Read Psalm 77:11 and paraphrase it here.

_____

_____

_____ ∎

Asaph said, "I will remember the deeds of the Lord." In Hebrew the word *remember* means "to call to mind again." This "calling to mind" isn't something that happens naturally. Asaph made a secret choice. He chose to turn from his depressing thoughts and walk on another path, the path of remembering who God is and what God has done in the past. He expressed his turnaround in another "I will" statement: "I will meditate on all your works and consider all your mighty deeds" (verse 12).

Friend, it is important that Asaph did not say, *I feel* but he said *I will*. His choices to remember and to meditate on what God had done were intentional choices. Asaph wrote an "I will remember" list of God's faithfulness in the past. This gave him hope that God would be faithful today and in the future.

 5. Read again Psalm 77:10–14 and ask God to show you how to write your "I will remember" list of God's faithfulness in your marriage and intimacy. Write it here or in your journal. As you write, we are praying for you.

_____

_____

_____

_____

_____

_____ ∎

"Lord, would You turn this dear wife's heart around so she can remember WHO You are and all You have done in the past. Let her remember Your faithfulness. Give her hope for today and for the future."

Debt-Free Intimacy

*"Over the long run, love's power to forgive
is stronger than hate's power to get even."*
—Dr. Lewis B. Smedes, *Forgive and Forget*

THEME:

Forgiveness is a secret, powerful choice that paves the way for deep intimacy.

THEME VERSE:

"Let all bitterness and wrath and anger and clamor and slander be put away from you, along with all malice. Be kind to one another, tender-hearted, forgiving each other, just as God in Christ also has forgiven you." (Ephesians 4:31–32 NASB)

If you have more than one child, try giving one a huge slice of cake when the other gets a sliver. Celebrate one's birthday with a party and ignore the other child's. Then get ready for the very predictable protest, "It's not fair!" You don't have to teach your children about fairness. They are born with the inclination to demand justice. It is part and parcel of the image of God who is righteous and just.

Paul says that the law of God is written on the human heart (see Romans 2:15). No matter your background, your culture, or your personality, you have an innate sense of justice. You hear of a man brutally raping a woman and your heart cries out for justice to be done. You wonder why a woman who is a virgin when she gets married can't enjoy sex while her friend who was promiscuous as a young woman has a great sex life. It's just not fair!

Our struggles to receive God's forgiveness, to forgive ourselves, and to extend forgiveness to another person (*especially* a husband) are all about justice.

"He doesn't deserve to be forgiven. It's just too much!"

"Why should I forgive him if he's likely just to do it again?"

"I will never feel free from the mistakes of my past. They are too terrible to forgive."

These are statements reflecting the demand for justice. Forgiveness is about debt, whether it is your sin or someone else's sin against you. There has been an offense and a payment must be made. It's only fair. It's righteous. It's just.

You slept with many men. You aborted a child or perhaps several. You've harbored anger and bitterness toward your husband for decades. Justice says that you deserve to suffer for your sins.

Your father abused you sexually or emotionally. Your mother did nothing to stop him. Your husband betrayed you with his choices. These people wounded you beyond expression. They deserve to be tried and sentenced to severe punishment!

How simple it is to say the words "I forgive you" when someone steps on your toe or sends you a belated birthday card. But the forgiveness involved in authentic intimacy is so deep, so raw, and so profound that it cannot be quickly offered or flippantly accepted. Sexual sins, ones you have committed and those committed against you, are among the most challenging to square with forgiveness. We see this in Sarah's journal.

When my husband, the one who vowed before God and a whole church full of people to love and cherish me forever,
When this man who shares my bed and intimately knows every inch of my body,
When this man I give my heart, my time, my body, my passion to,
When this man turns from my arms and embraces another,
IT IS BETRAYAL!
My heart is wounded, broken, bleeding
How could he????
How dare he?
How can I forgive him?
Why should I forgive him?

When your gut-wrenching pain comes from the most intimate sins and offenses of your life, it is natural for you to assume the burden of deciding and meting out justice. You know what he deserves and you want to see that he gets it.

The same applies to your sin. Somewhere along the road, you have judged yourself. You've measured your sin and decided your punishment. How much of life revolves around this justice? You sabotage your marriage because you have condemned yourself to an unhappy life. You hurt your body with penalties like junk food, nicotine, cutting, obesity, or alcohol to pay for the sins that seem to be buried so deep. And guilt . . . the ever-present emotional punishment that will never let you be free to enjoy the true love of God.

Then comes the reminder of forgiveness. Christ extends it to you and asks you to give it freely.

Bear with each other and forgive whatever grievances you may have against one another. Forgive as the Lord forgave you. (Colossians 3:13)

But it's not fair! Forgiveness seems to suggest that you shortcut and do away with justice. How does it make you feel to know that a murderer, rapist, or corporate thief has gotten away with a crime because he had a great lawyer? Your heart screams, "What about justice!" You may feel that same visceral response when it comes to forgiveness. How can God or anyone else suggest that the due penalty shouldn't be paid for these sins?

You must understand that the forgiveness God has called you to, for yourself and others, does not compete with justice. The loving Savior who hung on the cross is still the judge who is seated at the right hand of the Father. He is still the Righteous One who says that, "Everything done in secret will be exposed" (our paraphrase of Mark 4:22).

But this righteous judge has another name: Redeemer. He brings redemption for one reason—because He loves.

I AM FORGIVEN

DAY 1

Accepting the Cost of Forgiveness

Forgiveness presents us with a paradox: it is a free gift of God yet will cost you greatly to embrace it. Many Christians walk around with a cheap version of forgiveness. They accept the payment for sins in their minds and they may even be confident that they will someday be in heaven. However, they have never taken the costly journey to receive the Lord's forgiveness to the innermost places of the heart.

The beautiful woman in the gospel of Luke who worshiped at Jesus' feet is our guide to total forgiveness. Today we will use the example of what she relinquished to walk in the full forgiveness of Jesus.

♥ 1. Read Luke 7:36–50. Ask the Lord to speak directly to you through this recorded event in history. Write your thoughts here:

_____

_____

_____ ■

♥ 2. Forgiveness costs you your *passivity*.

a. In what ways did this dear woman fight through her passivity to get in Jesus' presence?

_____

_____

_____ ■

b. How have you been passive in your approach to know God's forgiveness?

_____

_____

_____ ■

c. How is the Lord asking you to actively pursue His presence?

_____

_____

_____ ■

3. Forgiveness costs you your *dignity*.

a. How do you see this woman abandoning her dignity to be at Jesus' feet?

_____

_____

_____ ■

b. What do Simon's thoughts in verse 39 tell you about this woman? What kind of sin do you imagine she was involved in?

_____

_____

_____ ■

c. How does your pride keep you from honestly answering the question "What kind of woman are you?"

_____

_____

_____ ■

♥ 4. Forgiveness costs you your *reputation*.

a. The woman in Luke 7 obviously had a sordid reputation. But by coming to Jesus, she broke every social custom. How did her actions put her under the scrutiny and criticism of others?

_____

_____

_____

_____

_____ ■

b. How has concern for your reputation kept you from knowing total forgiveness?

_____

_____

_____

_____

_____ ■

♥ 5. Forgiveness costs you your *unbelief*.
a. Read Luke 7:50 and write it here.

_____

_____

_____

_____

_____

_____ ■

Joy's story

Each day . . . I have been doing a lot of thinking about the passage in Luke 7. It is amazing to me how this woman's brokenness led her to worship Jesus. This woman's brokenness was a pathway that led her to an intimacy with Jesus that transcended to a level beyond the others in the room. I want that so badly. I want my brokenness to draw me closer to Christ, which goes hand in hand with being able to fellowship in His sufferings. Another thing I was thinking about was the men who were trying to tell Jesus who that woman was. The ways they responded to her made me imagine that maybe one of them or some of them had visited her in the silent brothel of her being. I also tried to think about this woman's background— maybe she was like me . . . severely abused as a child even to the point of having to worship Satan as a temple prostitute. If so, the beauty of trust and brokenness that shines forth as she worships the real Jesus is absolutely amazing.

b. This woman took great risk in coming to Jesus based on her faith—her belief that He would receive her and could cleanse her. While you may believe that Jesus can generically forgive some people, do you truly believe that He will receive and forgive all of *your* sins?

_____

_____

_____ ∎

The woman we have been intimately studying today entered the house of a Pharisee, seeking forgiveness and complete renewal. She was eager, desperate, and probably terrified. But the shackles of her sin and shame drove her to extreme measures—she risked all, brought her most treasured possession, and threw herself on the mercy of the Redeemer. You are this woman. The masks of your independence, accomplishments, and polished presentation can hide the fact that deep in your heart you are no less desperate to be redeemed. This woman left that house a new creation. Forgiveness and intimacy with Jesus was her new reality. Her abandoned pursuit of Jesus was the stake in the ground that marked her life as forever changed.

♥ 6. Today we invite you, in your desperation, to boldly burst through the door to where Jesus is. You will find that He has been waiting for you. Abandon your passivity, your dignity, your reputation, and your unbelief and pour your love at His feet. You do not come empty-handed to your Redeemer. He asks for the most precious thing from you—your brokenness and your love. Journal your thoughts here.

_____

_____

_____

_____

_____

_____ ∎

Our Redeemer,

May Your daughter walk away from this intimate encounter with You with the deep knowledge of the forgiveness that You have already purchased for her. Would You receive her offerings of praise and love and mark her as forever changed? May she be free to enjoy the deepest intimacy with You and with her husband, free from the shackles of guilt and shame. There is no name on earth or in heaven that can loosen these chains except for the name that is above every name . . . our Beloved Jesus.

Amen

Keeping No Record of Your Own Wrongs

Yesterday you meditated on receiving all of God's forgiveness for you—not just a forgiveness in your mind but down in your heart—a forgiveness that brings freedom! Forgiveness isn't just head knowledge but needs to seep deep down into the corners of your heart. Sometimes a woman knows God has forgiven her, but she just can't forgive herself. Freedom is not her daily delight.

Often we hear Christian women say, "I can forgive others but how can I ever forget what I have done? I know God forgives me but I can't forgive myself."

"I made the choice to abort my own child."

"Every time my husband and I make love, I'm visualizing the worship leader in my mind. Is that sick or what? And the worship leader's wife is my friend."

"I pleasure myself really often, just because I like to escape in my mind and body. What would my husband think if he knew."

God has been speaking a new thought about forgiveness to us. It is hidden in a simple, straightforward verse that is about love, not forgiveness. It is so simple that we pass over it when we read the beautiful love chapter in 1 Corinthians 13. We breeze right past the six words—six profound words that are not simple and that do speak of forgiveness. They are a key in how to forgive.

Love keeps no record of wrongs. (1 Corinthians 13:5)

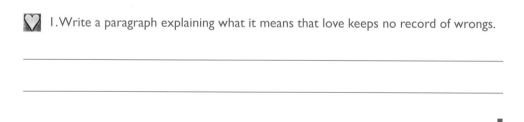

1. Write a paragraph explaining what it means that love keeps no record of wrongs.

_____

_____

_____ ■

In a previous lesson we studied the beautiful love chapter and challenged you to consider how you can love your husband in this selfless, sacrificial way. Some have said that the apex of this wonderful passage is the phrase found in verse 5: Love "keeps no record of wrongs." The Greek word that is translated as "no record" is *logizomai*, which means to reckon or impute.[1] In Romans 4:8, this Greek word is used: "Blessed is the man whose sin the Lord will never count against him."

Listen carefully—this is important! In God's sight your sin no longer exists. God does *not* keep a record of your wrongs. Receiving forgiveness does not mean letting yourself off the hook. It means acknowledging the reality that your sins have been paid for—in this life and in eternity!

> *Forgiving yourself may bring about the breakthrough you have been looking for. It could set you free in ways you have never before experienced. This is because we are afraid to forgive ourselves. We cling to fear as if it were a thing of value. The truth is, this kind of fear is no friend, but rather a fierce enemy. The very breath of Satan is behind the fear of forgiving ourselves.*—R.T. Kendall[2]

💜 2. How has the enemy taunted you about your sexual apathy or sexual sin?

_____

_____

_____ ■

Refusing to forgive yourself may be rooted in the **unbelief** that Jesus' sacrifice is total, not just for salvation but for walking in freedom.

💜 3. Read Psalm 103:8–14. What specifically do these verses say about the extent of God's forgiveness?

_____

_____

_____ ■

💜 4. Why does it require faith to believe that these statements apply to *you*?

_____

_____

_____ ■

A refusal to forgive yourself can also be rooted in **pride**. The human spirit is proud and independent. Inherently, you want to settle your own score, pay your own bill, make your own way. It just feels right to suffer for your sins by withholding pleasure or doing things that sabotage your chance for intimacy.

It takes total humility to embrace total forgiveness. It means throwing yourself on the Lord Jesus and acknowledging that there is nothing you can do to save yourself. Forgiveness and self-respect are incompatible.

♥ 5. Read Ephesians 2:8–9. How does walking in the freedom of forgiveness take away all boasting?

_____

_____

_____ ∎

A refusal to forgive yourself can also be rooted in **confusion** about the ongoing consequences of sin. Jamie's story is an example:

> During my teen years and early twenties, I was very rebellious. I slept with more men than I can remember and I am ashamed to say that I had three abortions. Drinking, drugs, and parties were my life. I didn't want anyone to interfere with my choices. When I was twenty-six, a friend invited me to a retreat and I gave my life to Christ. At that retreat, God changed my life. I was committed to purity until marriage and I gave up all my old ways. A few years later, God brought Craig, a wonderful Christian man, into my life. Not long into our marriage I discovered that I had contracted cervical cancer. To make a long story short, my case was very severe and I had to have a hysterectomy. The pain and grief this brought to me and my husband was terrible! I had robbed Craig of being a dad by my sin. This really has made me doubt God's forgiveness. If He really separates my sin as far as the east is from the west, why are we still living in punishment?

Forgiveness becomes hard to grasp when we, like Jamie, lump the spiritual and natural consequences of sin together, assuming they are one in the same. It is very important to understand the difference between spiritual redemption and God's work in the natural consequences of sin. While God may not remove the natural consequences of a sinful past, His forgiveness is still complete. Sin brings pain for us and for those around us. Although God may choose not to remove that pain, He offers to redeem it in a different way.

♥ 6. Read Romans 8:28. What does this verse say that God is able to do in _all_ things? What are the conditions of this promise?

_____

_____

_____ ∎

♥ 7. How can God redeem the consequences of sin (yours or others') for your good?

_____

_____

_____ ■

♥ 8. Fill in the blanks of this prayer:

Lord, I have had a very difficult time forgiving myself for:

_____

_____

_____ ■

Instead of trusting You, I have secretly made the choice to punish myself by:

_____

_____

_____ ■

Lord, the greatest barrier to my truly receiving Your forgiveness and keeping no record of my own wrongs is:

_____

_____

_____ ■

Oh, Redeemer, I give this barrier to You and ask You to help me walk in the freedom of Your forgiveness.

"I delight greatly in the Lord; my soul rejoices in my God. For he has clothed me with garments of salvation and arrayed me in a robe of righteousness . . ." Isaiah 61:10

DAY 3

The Power of Forgetting

The words you are about to read were written by a wife just like you. Beth had pledged herself to a Christian man, a pastor, whose struggle with pornography and eventually a sexual encounter destroyed their dreams. These few paragraphs are a sampling from her long journey to forgive the most intimate of betrayals.

Beth says: It wasn't the first time in our many years of marriage that I had been betrayed. He lied for a couple of weeks before coming clean and admitting the truth. We flew out of town to put some distance between us and the situation, and then soon discovered we would never go back to live in the home we had built just a couple of years before, and in which we had recently celebrated our granddaughter's second birthday. We were abruptly living a thousand miles away from our daughter who was seven months pregnant with our second granddaughter. The incomprehensible consequences unrelentingly continued to unfold, and ultimately led to the death of the dream we had shared and for which we had deeply sacrificed. The culmination was a violent expulsion of us and our precious family from our "promised land." This was devastation as I could never have imagined.

The hurt was so deep, and it threatened to trap me in a hardened fortress of offense, judgment, and self-righteousness. I didn't know where to put all of those feelings or how to live with them. I was tempted to unleash them on the one who had hurt me, to make him feel as bad as he had made me, and everyone else, feel.

Although we will be applying forgiveness to husbands for the next few days, you may have someone other than your husband to forgive. Perhaps it's a former boyfriend who hurt you or someone else who victimized you. Please apply the questions to that person the Lord is asking you to forgive.

How ... how ... HOW could I forgive such a wrong!? It was not only very personally against me at the core of my being but carried far-reaching destructive impact on those nearest and dearest to my heart.

Out of the healing, restoring womb of God's compassion for me in my pain emerged the compassion in my heart to forgive the one who was its cause. I could care for him as another human being, a fellow brother in Christ, who was hurting. I could see his intrinsic worth and value, bestowed on him by God when He gave Jesus to pay the price for this sin and its consequences. I knew that he had forgiveness from God. I could see that, except for the grace of God in my own life, I am capable of the same or even worse. I could see that my life was not my own and I was accountable to my Lord for how I managed my heart. I couldn't allow my soul to be hardened. I couldn't let this defeat and define me. With my life resembling a charred and smoking battlefield, amazingly, hope still lived! I realized that, as with Jesus on the cross, the way of victory over this evil would be the way of submission and obedience to my Father—the way of mercy and forgiveness.

This Scripture was one of my sources of inspiration, "Be kind and compassionate to one another, tender hearted, forgiving each other, just as in Christ God forgave you" (Ephesians 4:32).

Just as in Christ God forgave ME . . .

Under the shadow of what Jesus did for me and him, the possibility of the healing and restoration of our marriage was kept alive.

Beth's forgiveness cost far more than saying the three words, "I forgive you." It required her to forever lay down her rights to keep a record of what her husband's sin had stolen from her. When Beth chose to forgive, she gave up the power to remember her husband's offenses in order to gain a greater power: the power of forgetting.

Do you keep a list of your husband's wrongs against you? Are you saving the list so you can state your case against him in a heated argument? Do you use the list to remind yourself why this man should never again be trusted? "I'll remember that," you say, and you do remember. God wants you to let go of your mental record of wrongs.

A man who was telling his friend about an argument he'd had with his wife commented, "Oh, how I hate it. Every time we have an argument, she gets historical."

The friend replied, "You mean hysterical."

'No," he insisted, "I mean historical. Every time we argue she drags everything from the past and holds it against me!"

There is power in keeping a list. Mentally clinging to the litany of your husband's offenses against you promises to keep you safe. But the power is an illusion. In reality, your decision to keep a record of wrongs is a choice to thwart true intimacy. Keeping a record of wrongs is an act of the will, a choice not to love, not to forgive.

The glorious consequence of keeping no record of all wrongs is that you let go of the past and its effect on the present. You cast your care on God and trust Him to restore the wasted years. Truly, as Ruth Graham Bell has put it, "Marriage is the union of two good forgivers." Matthew chapter 18 has much to say about forgiveness.

♥ 1. Read Matthew 18:21–35. Listed below are God's attitudes toward you as pictured in this passage. Based upon His attitudes, write the corresponding attitude you should have toward your husband and others. The first example is done for you.

God's Attitude toward Me	My Attitude toward My Husband
God has forgiven me everything.	I need to forgive my husband.
God has forgiven me over and over.	
God forgives my worst sin.	
God forgives me quickly, never holding a grudge.	

♥ 2. God's forgiveness for you and your attitude toward your husband are inseparable. What does God say in Matthew 18 about the person who receives forgiveness but is unwilling to extend it?

_____

_____

_____ ∎

To forgive someone doesn't necessarily mean that you go back to life as usual. If a husband has been unfaithful to his wife many times, she is commanded by God to forgive him again and again. But forgiving him may not mean trusting him completely. He has to earn the trust that he has broken.

I (Juli) had a good friend named Brenda who was a judge. Brenda was not only a judge but an evangelist. She took every opportunity in the courtroom to talk about Jesus. After sentencing a man or woman to time in prison, she would often meet with them to tell them about the love and forgiveness of Jesus Christ.

Brenda's extension of God's forgiveness had nothing to do with the sentence that she gave the criminal. A person found guilty of murder, rape, or child abuse could receive God's full forgiveness but still be under the penalty of breaking the law. He would still have to spend many years proving to society that he was no longer a threat.

The same is true as it relates to forgiving a person. There is a distinction between forgiveness and reconciliation. Forgiveness is one-sided. It is saying in words and actions,

"I give up the right to hold a wrong against you." Reconciliation requires both people and is the restoration of trust in a relationship.

Romans 12:18 says, "as far as it depends on you, live at peace with everyone." Your job is to forgive and to be open to reconciliation.

 3. What do you think it looks like to offer forgiveness when the other person is not willing to change?

_____

_____

_____ ∎

Forgiveness is a secret choice—often known only to your Abba Father. It is a choice that delights His heart.

 4. Are you willing to write a prayer to God telling Him that you do not want to keep a record of your husband's wrongs? Ask Him for His help and guidance as you take this step.

_____

_____

_____ ∎

DAY 4
Time to Change Your Wardrobe

A friend of Clara Barton, founder of the American Red Cross, once reminded her of an especially cruel thing that had been done to her years before. But Miss Barton seemed not to recall it. "Don't you remember it?" her friend asked.

"No," came the reply, "I distinctly remember forgetting it."[3]

We love this story about Clara Barton as it shows clearly that forgiveness is a secret choice. We pray that you have seen this as you've studied God's Word this week. But how do you forgive? What does it practically look like to walk out forgiveness after you have made the choice to do it?

Let us share from the theme verses—our favorite verses about forgiveness. The apostle Paul's statement in Ephesians 4:31–32 is very clear; you are commanded to change the clothes you wear.

Strip Off! "Let all bitterness and wrath and anger and clamor and slander be put away from you, along with all malice" (Ephesians 4:31 NASB).

Put On! "Be kind to one another, tender-hearted, forgiving each other, just as God in Christ also has forgiven you" (Ephesians 4:32 NASB).

These verses clearly say you choose between two kinds of clothing. One common piece of advice in the work world is, "Dress for the job you want, not for the job you have!" We encourage you to dress for the marriage you want, not for the marriage you have. You choose to strip off your old wardrobe because it no longer represents who you are becoming.

♥ 1. Read Ephesians 4:31 again. List the six pieces of clothing you are to strip off and write your personal definition of each one.

_____

_____

_____

_____

_____

_____

_____

_____ ∎

♥ 2. Which piece of clothing is the most difficult for you to "strip off"?

_____

_____

_____ ∎

Strip yourselves of your old selfish, angry ways of relating. Instead there must be a spiritual renewal of your thoughts and attitudes (our paraphrase of Ephesians 4:23). And what does your new wardrobe look like? Three beautiful garments: kindness, compassion, and forgiveness.

Will you choose God's new wardrobe? Its shades of kindness, compassion, and forgiveness make your skin pop—your eyes sparkle. It fits like a fashion designer outfit, handcrafted just for you.

♥ 3. List your three new pieces of clothing in Ephesians 4:32, and give a definition of each one.

_____

_____

_____

_____

_____

_____

_____ ■

♥ 4. Which one is your "strong suit" (easiest for you to wear)?

_____

_____

_____ ■

♥ 5. Which one is the most difficult for you to "put on"? Why do you think this is hard for you?

_____

_____

_____ ■

When you get new clothes, you don't keep them in the closet. You want to wear them and show them off! It's time for a fashion show. When you put on the garments of Christ, you wear them by acting out forgiveness. Deliberate actions based on forgiveness put a stake in the ground, reminding you forever what you have chosen to forget.

♥ 6. Below are a few choices for how you can wear your new clothes. Choose one to do this week.

Write a letter of forgiveness

Write a letter of forgiveness or create an email card. You can take your husband out for a special evening and share your heart of forgiveness with him.

Like Winston Churchill, let your fingers do your forgiving

At a dinner party one night Lady Churchill was seated across the table from Sir Winston, who kept making his hand walk up and down—two fingers bent at the knuckles. The fingers appeared to be walking toward Lady Churchill. Finally, her dinner partner asked, "Why is Sir Winston looking at you so wistfully, and whatever is he doing with those two knuckles on the table?" "That's simple," she replied. "We had a mild quarrel before we left home, and he is indicating it's his fault and he's on his knees to me in abject apology."[4]

Throw the rock of bitterness away

When you sense your heart is holding on to bitterness and anger, go outside and find a quiet place alone, fall to your knees, and tell your Father what He already knows: *Forgive me for hanging on in my heart. I'm throwing off the anger and bitter feelings toward my husband.* Pick up a rock and name it bitterness. Throw the rock as far as you can throw and tell God you are banishing bitterness.

Exchange your anger with prayer

Stormie Omartian, author of *The Power of a Praying Wife*, says, "Something amazing happens to your heart when you pray for your husband. The hardness melts. You become able to get beyond the hurts, and forgive. It's miraculous! It happens because when we pray we enter into the presence of God and He fills us with His Spirit of love. When you pray for your husband, the love of God will grow in your heart for him."[5]

May your marriage truly be the union of two good forgivers!

DAY 5

The Secret Place: A Fragrant Offering

This week, we have challenged you to walk in forgiveness—both in the forgiveness you accept through Jesus and the forgiveness He asks you to extend to those who have hurt you. We pray that God has done a deep work in your heart. If you have taken steps to become a woman marked by forgiveness, you won't be able to hide it for long. People around you will begin to notice it—the fragrance of forgiveness.

In the message, we introduced you to two women who lived thousands of years apart but had one thing in common. They both took a dramatic step to seal their choice to walk in forgiveness through an anointing ceremony. You got to know the first woman through studying Luke 7.

♥ 1. Read Luke 7:38. What did the woman pour on Jesus' feet? How do you think this changed the environment of the room?

_____

_____

_____ ■

Linda shared with you the story of the second woman. Remember the forgiveness anointing? Can you imagine the fragrance that filled the room (physically and spiritually) as this precious woman anointed her husband, cementing forgiveness and healing? Forgiveness can be a form of worship that invites the scent of our Lord to fill every corner of your life and home.

♥ 2. Read 2 Corinthians 2:14–15. What does this passage say about how the fragrance Christ can spread through us?

_____

_____

_____ ■

♥ 3. Read Ephesians 5:1–2. How does this passage link a "life of love" as a fragrant offering and sacrifice to God?

_____

_____

_____ ■

This week may have prompted some difficult choices for you. Perhaps studying forgiveness has resurrected events and feelings that have long been buried. The Lord is showing you how to walk in greater freedom through the doorway of forgiveness. Your choice to accept His forgiveness and extend it to another may be a costly one. Whether it is a sacrifice of pouring out the perfume of your heart on Jesus' feet or a sacrifice of anointing another with undeserved love, your choice to forgive can be a fragrant offering of worship to the Lord.

4. Write a prayer of response, asking the Lord specifically how to fill your life and home with the beautiful fragrance of forgiveness.

FORGIVE

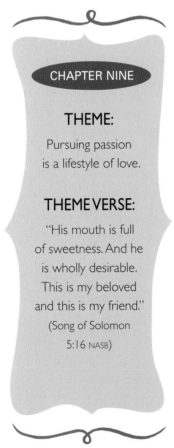

The Passion Priority

Just because we write books on sex, don't assume that we don't struggle to make intimacy a priority in marriage ourselves. I, Linda, will never forget a surprising phone call I received. A woman called and said, "I just didn't know when to call you because I know what you and your husband do all the time." I told Jody about the conversation. His comment? "I wish!"

So no—Jody and I don't make love all day. In fact, there are times for both Juli and me when passion is not high on our priority list. One secret we've learned is:

> The desire for intimacy is a result of making it a priority, not the other way around.

Now the fun begins. You get to take a short passion quiz to help you think honestly about where passion ranks on your list of priorities.

QUIZ:

1. My husband and I have at least two dates every month. Y ☐ N ☐

2. I often say no to worthy things in order to say yes to my husband. Y ☐ N ☐

3. My husband and I have at least one weekend getaway by ourselves a year. Y ☐ N ☐

4. We do not have a television in our bedroom. Y ☐ N ☐

5. My husband and I have talked about how we can carve out time for intimacy. Y ☐ N ☐

CHAPTER NINE

THEME:

Pursuing passion
is a lifestyle of love.

THEME VERSE:

"His mouth is full
of sweetness. And he
is wholly desirable.
This is my beloved
and this is my friend."
(Song of Solomon
5:16 NASB)

6. Our kids know never to walk into our bedroom without knocking (or visit our house without calling). Y ☐   N ☐

7. My husband and I have a secret code to ask for intimacy. Y ☐   N ☐

8. If several days go by without intimacy, one of us is sure to mention it as a concern. Y ☐   N ☐

9. Most of our sexual encounters are not quickies. Y ☐   N ☐

10. Our sex life is better now than it was a year ago. Y ☐   N ☐

HOW DID YOU SCORE?

Yes to eight or more questions—you are smokin' hot!

Yes to five to seven questions—not bad.

Yes to fewer than five questions—it's time to make passion a priority.

Think with us about making passion more of a priority in your life. The dictionary definition of priority is "Precedence, especially established by order of importance or urgency." So . . . what does it mean to you that passion with your husband is to be "established by order of importance or urgency"? We asked women what the Passion Priority meant to them:

"I think it means making time to have sex . . . but it's just not possible—there's too much to do with work, kids, house, EVERYTHING!"

"Sex should be high on my list of important items."

"Makes me think—I spend more time on food for him than on exciting sex. I think I know what he would rather have."

"Passion priority means that our sex life goes beyond quickies."

"Putting a priority stamp on your passion means fun, laughter, flirting, encouraging each other, exploring life together, and yes, getting naked . . ."

DAY 1

Putting Passion on Your Calendar

"Teach us to number our days aright, that we may gain a heart of wisdom." (Psalm 90:12)

Marty, a friend of ours, took these words from Moses seriously. She actually totaled up the number of days she would have left on earth if she lives to be seventy. Marty was thirty at the time and discovered that the remaining forty years would give her 14,600 days. Being a superachiever, Marty resolved to live each day to the fullest. But, like most of us, her zeal lasted about a week, and then she forgot about it. When she again read Psalm 90 and numbered her days, several years had passed and in shock Marty discovered she had only 12,000 days remaining. *Where did they go? What did I do with those 2,600 days?*

What do we do with our days? Women today are scattered, running from one role to another. Mom shoves food in kids. Wife kisses husband goodbye. Mom drives car pool. Teacher, Nurse, Administrator races to work. Over lunch, Christian Friend prays with a woman whose husband just left her. Then back to her day job. Mom and Wife cook dinner. Mom helps with homework, gets kids in bed. Wife slips in bed exhausted, hoping that she doesn't have to go into Lover mode.

Sexual intimacy with your husband should not be a luxury or an option only if you both have enough time and energy. It also wasn't designed to be just a wifely duty. If you ever want your love life to be something you look forward to, that priority must be reflected on your calendar.

💜 1. Based on your responses to the passion quiz, what do you think is the greatest barrier to making passion a priority on your calendar?

_____

_____

_____ ∎

Time management coaches often talk about the danger of allowing the "urgent" to override the "important." Although passion in your marriage is important, it may not be urgent. You can put it on the shelf for weeks and months while you attend to more urgent matters like a sick child, a nonworking washing machine, a work deadline, or the dreaded school science project. In the meantime, the spark that you and your husband once enjoyed is slowly fading.

I can't shut my mind off until everything around the house is done. Once I get the kids to bed, my mind shifts to the dishes in the sink, getting everything organized for tomorrow, and the laundry in the dryer that will be wrinkled if I don't fold it now.—Tori

The laundry and dishes may be done and Tori may feel ready for tomorrow but what is happening to her marriage as she continually says yes to the urgent at the expense of the important?

💜 2. What "urgent" but nonessential things do you often choose over investing in passion in your marriage?

_____

_____

_____ ∎

♥ 3. Describe why passion is an important part of your life but not urgent.

_____

_____

_____

_____

_____ ▪

♥ 4. In Psalm 90:12, Moses asks the Lord to teach him to remember his life is fleeting so that he can live wisely. Today, we would like for you to number your days. Of course, none of us are guaranteed even one more day. But assuming that you and your husband will both live to seventy, eighty, or even ninety, how many days do you have left to be husband and wife?

_____

_____ ▪

♥ 5. If you were to live the rest of your days responding to the urgent things of life and neglecting the priority of passion, what regrets might you have at the end of your days?

_____

_____

_____ ▪

GETTING PERSONAL WITH *Linda*

As I look back on almost fifty years of marriage, I am filled with thankfulness to God. He burned into my heart that intimacy with Jody needed to be a priority in my lifestyle. Did I do this perfectly every year of our marriage? Of course not. But I consistently made secret choices to make passion a priority. I don't regret spending an afternoon making love with my husband instead of cleaning up a messy house. I don't regret trying over and over again to spend a weekend alone with my husband when it seemed like it was too much work. I don't regret swallowing embarrassment and saying or doing what my husband asked me to try because it made his face light up with pleasure.

One way to make passion a priority is to actually put it on your calendar. Perhaps you are thinking, *Schedule sex? Boring!* It doesn't have to be. In fact, scheduled sex can be even more exciting because it gives you time to prepare and plan. Take Tim and Carrie for example. On their calendars are days circled in red pen, reminding them of urgent passion appointments. Carrie says the anticipation and fun emails—"Don't forget our important meeting at 6:40 p.m. today!"—make scheduled sex even better than the spontaneous variety. So try it, you might like it.

GETTING PERSONAL WITH *Juli*

My life is busy. Kids, work, housework, ministry . . . I've struggled over the years knowing how to balance it all and making passion in my marriage a priority. It isn't that I didn't love Mike or enjoy our relationship. I just had no time or energy. During a few years of our marriage, I began to dread intimacy like a chore. It was right up there with doing the dishes or taking out the trash. It had become just one more thing that *had* to be done. Intimacy with my husband isn't like that anymore. What changed? Frankly, a lot. One of the biggest changes was learning that being my husband's "lover" isn't just another role for me. It isn't just one more thing to juggle or one more hat to put on at the end of the day. It is a lifestyle that is the overflow of my love for God. I shared in the message about how God prompted me to initiate sex with my husband while I was reading my Bible in The Secret Place with the Lord. This has happened many times. God asked me to put my Bible aside and put my devotion for Him into action. Once I really started to understand that my attitude about passion was important to God, I made it a priority in my thinking and how I approached my marriage. It took awhile for this to filter down to my feelings but it eventually did and changed everything!

Putting Passion in Your Mind

The ability to enjoy mental imagery can be used to expand and enjoy all aspects of your life, including lovemaking."[1]

Do you know that your mind is by far your most important sexual organ? Dr. Douglas Rosenau, theologian and Christian sex therapist, says, "Sex is 80 percent imagination and mind and 20 percent friction."[2] Your mind is the control center for your sexual feelings.

For many wives, the greatest deterrent to enjoying regular sex is that they just can't get their mind ready. After a day of racing from one demand to the next, thinking about passion seems impossible.

Think back. When was the last time you set your mind on making passion a priority? Your anniversary or maybe your last vacation? We want to help you realize that passion can be a recurring priority in your mind.

♥ 1. Write Romans 12:2 here. Paraphrase it in your own words.

_____

_____

_____

_____

_____

_____

_____

_____ ∎

We love how the New Living Translation renders this verse:

Let God transform you into a new person by changing the way you think.

Now apply that: let God transform you into a new wife by changing the way you think! We've spent weeks in this study working to get the junk about sex out of your mind. Now it's time to plant some positive, SHM thoughts.

The first step to renewing your mind is to get God's Word into your mind. Memorizing God's Word sets your mind on what God desires. Cynthia Heald says it this way: "Memorizing God's Word increases the Holy Spirit's vocabulary in your mind."[3] And you need the Holy Spirit's vocabulary to grow regarding making passion a priority!

Casey took Proverbs 5:19 and wrote this personalized Scripture prayer.

God, thank You that You say I am to be like a graceful and beautiful deer to my husband, that my breasts are to satisfy him at all times. God, show me how to be a creative and sensuous lover to him, how to use my breasts, my body, to give him pleasure. I want him to be intoxicated and exhilarated with my skill as a lover.

We pray you are serious about memorizing and meditating on God's Word because when you do, new passion patterns blossom in your mind. And as God's Word filters down to your heart, you begin to act differently. You begin to act passionately!

We see the young bride in Song of Solomon using her mind to shift her body into sexual gear. Solomon and his bride had just had a fight about sex. He came after midnight to make love and she rejected him. (Sounds like it happened today . . .) Solomon left in a huff and SHM felt guilty. What did she do? She began to dwell on her husband's body . . . his naked, aroused body.

GETTING PERSONAL WITH *Linda*

How have I transformed my mind? My parents' marriage ended in divorce because my dad was an abusive alcoholic. I had junk in my mind from my family home, from some wrong choices in college. As a new Christian and new bride, I wanted my mind filled with God's truth about passion. So I memorized lots of verses and passages about the kind of lover I wanted to be. One passage I planted in my mind was Proverbs 5:15–19. I memorized it, then I meditated on it and asked God to make it come alive to me. Next I personalized the passage back to God in prayer. My prayer went something like this:

God, thank You for the beautiful imagery of water—You say Jody is to come to my body to be filled up—that my sexual love is to be like refreshing, cool water to a thirsty man. I love this, Lord, and I want it to be true . . . I want to be a fountain of blessing for Jody. I long for him to be intoxicated with my sexual love. Oh Lord, make Your Word my reality. I long to be a captivating lover!

2. Read Song of Solomon 5:10–16.

The author of *Intimate Allies*, who is an Old Testament scholar, makes this statement about the nature of SHM's thinking. "After commenting on his strong arms, she then describes a part of his body as polished ivory. Most English translations hesitate in this verse. The Hebrew is quite erotic, and most translators cannot bring themselves to bring out the obvious meaning. The smooth and expensively ornamented tusk of ivory is a loving description of her husband's erect penis."[4]

Are you shocked God included a picture of a wife imagining her husband's naked, aroused body in His Holy Word? (Note the important word, *husband*.) God not only gives you permission to dwell on your husband's body, He encourages it!

How do I, Linda, use my mind to shift my body into sexual gear? Stored in my mind are almost fifty years of sexual memories with Jody, a storehouse of treasures. When sex is the last thing on my mind but very much on his mind, I pull out the memories and reflect on: A time of great intimacy. A time of great laughter and fun. A time of exquisite pleasure.

 3. What specifically helps you to get your mind focused on being passionate with your husband?

One smart wife said that when her heart, mind, and body were a million miles away from lovemaking, she would go through a little ceremony of lighting the many candles in their bedroom. By the fifth candle, her mind and heart were transformed.

Candle 1: *Lord, please light a fire in my mind for my husband.*
Candle 2: *Lord, ignite a fire in my heart for him.*
Candle 3: *Oh God, light a fire in my body . . . my body is dead.*
Candle 4: *My Lord, remind me, please, of all the reasons I love him.*
Candle 5: *Lord, thank You that I am my beloved's and his desire is for me.*

DAY 3
Putting Passion in Your Body

You know the traditional wedding vows. But we bet you don't know this portion of an older Anglican wedding vow. One lover says to the other:

With my body I thee worship
My body will adore you
Your body alone will I cherish
I will with my body declare your worth.[5]

These words are beautiful. It is as if the bride's body is shrouded with holiness. But would a 21st-century bride snicker if she said, "My body will adore you"? We think she might, as we women have trouble thinking positive thoughts about our bodies.

We want to begin today's lesson by asking you a question right out of the gate.

♥ 1. How important do you think your body is to sexual fulfillment? Why?

_____

_____

_____ ∎

Your body is the primary tool through which you give and receive sexual pleasure. We've met many women for whom issues related to body were the primary obstacles to a great sex life. Here are a few examples:

"I just can't feel sexy with my husband with the way I look. Every time my husband wants to touch me, I feel self-conscious about my weight. I can't make love with the lights on because all I can think about is the roll around my middle."

"I've never felt sexy because my breasts are small. I'm embarrassed to admit that I often fantasize during sex about having large breasts. My husband says my body is pleasing to him, but I just don't believe him."

"My husband is very critical about my appearance ever since I had children. I just can't seem to drop the baby weight. He wants me to be back to a size 4 and is always dropping hints that I need to work out."

These women's comments represent a lot of pain. Most women can relate to the insecurities and frustrations expressed here. Whether you are tall or short, thin or heavy, pale or dark, there is probably something you don't like about your body. Even the beautiful Smokin' Hot Mama had body image issues!

♥ 2. Paraphrase Song 1:5–6.

_____

_____

_____ ∎

SHM felt insecure about her body just like you do. But something happened that changed her insecurity into freedom. As you've read through Song of Solomon this week, you've seen that SHM displayed her body for her husband to see. He talks about her breasts over and over (Song 4:5; 7:3; 7:7). Somehow, she became a confident lover—sure that her body could captivate her husband. The Song doesn't tell us exactly how this happened but we have a few guesses.

"After giving birth to three nine-pound boys, my stomach is not what it used to be. I am not exaggerating when I say that it looks like a rumpled paper bag. Just the other day, one of my boys saw my stomach and pulled back like he had just seen Gollum from *The Lord of the Rings*. My husband used to love my stomach. Once upon a time, he praised me like Solomon for how flat and flawless it was. Naturally, my post-childbirth midsection became a source of insecurity for me. I didn't want Mike to see or touch my stomach during intimacy. Once I shared this with Mike, he kissed my wrinkly stomach and said, 'I love your stomach, marks and all. It is what carried our three little boys.' I could either accept his affirmation or hang on to my insecurity."[6]

SHM chose to believe the compliments her husband gave her. Throughout the song, we see Solomon going into great detail about how he loves his wife's body. Instead of arguing with him, she gratefully receives his praise. A wife can create a self-fulfilling prophecy by always speaking negatively about her own body and even refuting her husband's compliments. Every time her husband says something nice about her body, she refutes it with negative thoughts or statements like, "Seriously? How could I turn you on? Have you seen how flabby I am?" Eventually, he stops complimenting her.

🖤 3. How do you respond when your husband compliments you about your body?

_____

_____

_____

_____

_____ ∎

We also believe that SHM made the choice to not dwell on her body inadequacies but on how to use her body skillfully to bring intoxicating ecstasy to her husband. She realized that her body could do more than just provide her husband something to look at. It could also bring her husband great pleasure. SHM was a smart wife. So is Carolyn.

Carolyn, a wife married forty years, captured this freedom: "I have saggy breasts, varicose veins, and a leftover tummy from three babies, but as my body has fallen, my expertise as a lover has risen! I think my dear husband still sees my body as it was because of the pleasure he receives from it."

Listen carefully . . . this is key!

It's not what you have but what you do with what you have!

Did you get that? Read it again. It is *really* important!

♥ 4. Look through SOS and give some examples of how Smokin' Hot Mama delighted her husband with her body.

_____

_____

_____ ▪

♥ 5. Will you make a secret choice before God to say no to insecurity about your body and yes to delighting your husband with your body? Write your secret choice to God here or in your journal.

_____

_____

_____ ▪

DAY 4

A Gift Exchange

In the session, we talked about giving your body as a gift to your husband. You laughed about Kathy wrapping herself in a bow to fulfill 1 Corinthians 7:4. Perhaps you gulped as you laughed. Think about the different emotions you feel when you give someone a gift. There are some gifts that you have shopped for and saved for. You are so excited to give it because you just _know_ how much the person is going to love it. It's the perfect gift! You think, _Open it now! I can't wait to see your face! You're going to be so happy when you see what I got you!_

Then there are other gifts. Like the time you forgot a friend's birthday and you hunted around the house for something to give, just so you wouldn't show up empty-handed. You put little thought or effort into the gift and you even offered apologies as you gave it. "It's just something little." What you were really thinking was, _Don't get your hopes up. Please, don't even say the obligatory thank-you because I know you won't like it._

♥ 1. Okay. Here's a tough question. If you viewed your body as a gift you give to your husband, what kind of gift is it? Put into words what you are thinking as you give this gift.

_____

_____

_____ ▪

♥ 2. What kind of gift would you like to be giving your husband?

_____

_____

_____ ■

You do not have to have a perfect body in order to give your husband a gift he will _love_! In fact, most women who become obsessed with having a perfect body are not great lovers. They spend far more time thinking about themselves than they spend thinking about how to be pleasing to their husbands! Too much focus on physical appearance is rooted in pride and insecurity, not in confident servanthood.

It's time to ask you an important question. Have you given your body as a gift to your husband?

♥ 3. Write 1 Corinthians 7:3–5 here.

_____

_____

_____

_____

_____

_____

_____

_____ ■

This important passage teaches every husband and wife about why God says to make passion a priority in marriage. In verse 3 you see the principle of need. Both husbands and wives have sexual needs. God's Word _commands_—it does not _suggest_—that we meet our spouse's sexual needs.

♥ 4. Why do you believe God commands a wife to meet her husband's sexual needs?

_____

_____

_____ ■

In verse 4 you see the principle of *authority*. Do you see the beauty of the gift exchange? Each partner gives up the right to his or her own body and turns that authority over to the other. This gift exchange is a beautiful thing. The *Bible Knowledge Commentary* says this about 1 Corinthians 7:3–4: "Paul stressed the equality and reciprocity of the husband and wife's sexual relationship by emphasizing the responsibilities of each to satisfy the other."[7] We like the words "equality" and "reciprocity" as these two things are what sexual intimacy in marriage is all about.

♥ 5. What does it mean to you that you have authority over your husband's body and he has authority over yours?

_____

_____

_____ ▪

In verse 5 you see the principles of *habit*. Sexual fulfillment isn't supposed to only happen on vacation, on your anniversary, or when you have enough energy. It is designed to be a regular part of marriage.

♥ 6. What reasons do you see in verse 5 for abstaining from making passion a priority?

_____

_____

_____ ▪

For a wife to give authority of her body to her husband is to say:

I entrust my body to you—it is no longer mine but yours.

I yield my body freely as a vessel to give and receive love.

I am forever only yours—all of me.

You can be creative in how you choose to give your husband the gift of your body.

Melody more than shocked her husband when she presented her body in a purple bow on their twentieth anniversary. He liked the shock!

Deborah donned her wedding dress and said, "Let's start over . . . I want to do it right."

Janeen felt only a bow went too far for her, so she pinned a yellow bow to her nightgown.

Jessica planned a whole romantic weekend away that included lovely music, candles, and a walk by the river. The menu of special food delighted their senses, and the dessert was Jessica, wrapped in a chocolate adorned ribbon!

Ask the Lord to show you your special, individual, creative way to give your body as a gift to your husband.

DAY 5

The Secret Place: Offer a Sacrifice of Thanksgiving

We wonder if the questions asked this week make you feel tired? Put passion on your calendar. Put passion in your mind, in your body, and set the stage for passion. Look back over the first four days of study and ask, "Lord, what about this is hard for me?" Maybe it is body issues or mind issues or just plain not wanting to make passion a priority.

If your husband were more understanding, more fun, more passionate, more *anything* you wouldn't have to work so hard at passion!

We're sure your husband should be many things he's not, but we know and you know that you can only make choices for yourself. As you come to The Secret Place, will you make the secret choice to offer a sacrifice of thanksgiving?

1. Write Psalm 50:14–15 here. What do you learn about a sacrifice of thanksgiving in these verses?

_____

_____

_____

_____

_____

_____

2. Write Psalm 50:23 here. What additional information does this give you?

_____

_____

_____

_____

_____

_____

Many of us need to give thanks for the body we live in. Others just need to thank God that they have a husband to thank God for. But some wives say, "I feel fake thanking God when I just don't feel thankful." Dr. John Mitchell, cofounder of Multnomah University, responds to that thought this way: "To give thanks when you don't feel like it is not hypocrisy; it's obedience."[8]

💜 **3. Paraphrase Hebrews 13:15 here. What words stand out to you in this verse?**

_____

_____

_____ ■

In Hebrews 13:5, thanksgiving and praise are linked together as a sacrifice. We love what Merlin Carothers says about this:

> I have come to believe that the prayer of praise is the highest form of communion with God, and one that always releases a great deal of power into our lives. Praising Him is not something we do because we feel good; rather it is an act of obedience. Often the prayer of praise is done in sheer teeth-gritting willpower; yet when we persist in it, somehow the power of God is released into us and into the situation.[9]

So let us ask you: Do you need the power of God released in your sexual intimacy?

"I need God's power to overtake my mind, which so needs to be renewed!"—Wendy

"I need God's power to change my crummy attitude about making passion a priority." —Shelly

"I desperately need God's power to give me a new view of my body —I hate my body."—Maria

Friend, what do you need?

💜 **4. Will you honestly write a letter to God asking for His help with your need? Write it here or in your journal.**

_____

_____

_____

_____

_____

_____ ■

5. Write a prayer to God expressing your sacrifice of thanksgiving to Him.

_____

_____

_____

_____ ▪

Additional Day

If Your Sexual Desire Is Greater than Your Husband's

Perhaps the topic this week is hurtful to you. _You_ would love to make passion a priority but your husband never does. As we teach women about sexual intimacy, a growing number of them are asking, "What do I do if my husband isn't interested in sex?"

If you are one of the many women asking this question, you may wonder what's wrong with you and why your husband seems to not be attracted to you. You may even question your femininity and sexuality. You might also wonder if your sex drive is abnormal. Other wives seem bent on avoiding sex; is there something wrong with you if you actually crave it?

Other days, you probably shift from shame to blame, feeling angry with your husband for his seeming inability or unwillingness to meet your needs for love, affirmation, and sexual fulfillment. You desperately want to be cherished and embraced by your husband. His disinterest feels like a total rejection of who you are as a wife and a woman.

If this describes your marriage, we hope this extra day of homework will be a source of encouragement and help for you.

Throughout _Passion Pursuit,_ you have learned that every couple has challenges in the bedroom. Some have to battle through the wounds of sexual abuse or rebuild trust because of past choices. Others have physical problems that make sex painful or impossible. Throughout this course, we have encouraged you to develop skills that will help you address many of these problems, including the challenge of a husband not interested in sex.

Bring It before the Lord

God cares about your sexual relationship with your husband. He knows intimately the challenges you face, the rejection you feel, and the fears you harbor. But perhaps you haven't felt free to express these to Him and to ask for His wisdom.

♥ 1. Express your feelings to the Lord in the space below (or in a separate journal) about how your husband's lack of interest in sexual intimacy has impacted you. Ask Him for His strength and wisdom to know how to address this challenge in a way that builds intimacy.

_____

_____

_____

_____

_____

_____

_____

_____ ■

Take Away the Shame

There are many, many couples who are in your situation. Don't complicate the issue by piling on blame and shame. You and your husband are *not* abnormal. Every couple has challenges, and this happens to be yours. Be sure that your attitude and communication on this topic are not laden with blame (there's something wrong with you) or shame (there's something wrong with me).

♥ 2. Have you ever felt ashamed that you have sexual needs that are not met by your husband?

_____

_____

_____ ■

♥ 3. This week and in other parts of this study, you looked at Paul's teaching in I Corinthians 7:3– 4. What does this passage say about your sexual needs?

_____

_____

_____ ■

Work Together to Remove Obstacles

There are many reasons why a guy may have a low sex drive or avoid sex. It is key to identify if there is an underlying issue that can be resolved. If your husband desires sex less than once a week, you may want to consider the following potential reasons:

- Physical issues such as thyroid disease, low testosterone levels, medications that interfere with sex drive or performance, obesity, or exhaustion.

- Emotional roadblocks like depression or chronic stress. Sexual abuse can also be a hidden reason a man avoids intimacy.

- Fear of failure. Consider that many men avoid sex with their wives because of fear of failure.

- Relationship dynamics. In some cases, a man who feels very passive in his marriage will also be passive sexually. If you tend to be dominant or controlling emotionally, this may have an impact on how your husband responds to you sexually.

- Other outlets. If a man is involved in pornography or other sexual outlets, he is likely to find it difficult to respond sexually to his wife. Pornography offers instant gratification to highly erotic material while marital sex requires patience and self-control. It is critical that this obstacle be removed for you to establish a healthy sexual relationship with your husband. Another possible reason your husband may not be interested in sex is gender confusion or a homosexual orientation. Obviously, this presents a very painful and difficult problem that has ramifications for many aspects of your marriage. If you suspect this might be an issue, please seek professional and spiritual guidance.

Find Ways of Connecting Intimately

Express to your husband your desire to be close to him, within the context of wanting to understand how your desire for sex impacts him. Perhaps you and your husband have been in a pattern of rejection. You initiate or hint for intimacy and he turns you down.

 You get angry and avoid him. If you are in this cycle, work to find ways of connecting with your husband to which he is more likely to respond. For example, if he has a fear of failure, learn to engage in sexual touch that doesn't have to lead to intercourse. Let him know that he can please you sexually in many ways. If you tend to be the dominant one in the relationship, think of how to connect with him in ways that build his emotional confidence.

♥ 4. What are some ways you can approach your husband intimately without repeating the pattern of rejection?

_____

_____

_____

_____

_____

_____ ∎

Consider How to Become a Servant Lover

Remember the challenge in week 5 to become a servant lover through your differences? God is concerned about your sexual needs and intimacy in your marriage. But He is also concerned about what kind of lover you are becoming. A difference in desire like yours can be fertile ground for resentment and bitterness to grow. It can also create walls of shame that keep you and your husband from sharing other forms of intimacy like talking and having fun.

♥ **5. How do you think the Lord could use your unique situation to teach you to love as He loves?**

_____

_____

_____

_____

_____

_____ ∎

Becoming a Smokin' Hot Mama

CHAPTER TEN

THEME:

God wants you
to become a
Smokin' Hot Mama.

THEME VERSE:

"I am my lover's,
and my lover is mine."
(Song of Solomon
6:3 NLT)

This is the chapter you have been waiting for and working toward: becoming a Smokin' Hot Mama! You have faithfully endured ten weeks of teaching and homework because you have a desire. You have determined to do what it takes to improve sexual intimacy in your marriage.

So how do you go from a ho-hum sex life to toe-curling, *wow!* intimacy? You are not the only woman asking this question. Have you noticed how many of the grocery store magazines have sex advice advertised on the front cover? These magazines target women.

If you are looking for help, you can walk right past the women's magazines and romance novels. These may offer quick tips to immediate pleasure, but in the long run, they steal from the authentic intimacy your heart desires. God has given you His Holy Spirit–inspired resource.

Your Great God, your King, the Lover of your Soul, desires to take you gently by the hand and lead you, His precious daughter, into all it means for *you* to become a Smokin' Hot Mama. We hope that the last nine weeks have shown you the importance God places on pursuing passion. He not only gives you permission to be a passionate wife but is pleased as you seek to become a Smokin' Hot Mama to your husband. As we have said throughout this study, pursuing passion in marriage is an important part of reclaiming from the enemy God's beautiful gift of sexuality.

This week's study will be different than the preceding nine weeks. Every week you have studied God's Word at home and thought about how to apply it to your marriage. You've discussed questions and thoughts with the women in your small group. This week, what you discover will only be between you and your husband. It's time to take what you have learned and bring it into the intimacy of your marriage.

DAY 1

Creativity: The SHM Kind

One of the most obvious things we can learn from SHM is that sex was not boring in her marriage. She was creative! She used her imagination to keep intimacy in her marriage exciting. Her creativity included planning a fun escape for her and her husband.

1. Read Song of Solomon 7:11–13 and paraphrase it here.

_____

_____

_____

_____

_____

_____

_____

2. What do you think SHM meant when she told her husband she had new and old choice fruits saved up for him, her lover?

_____

_____

_____

3. What kind of sexual "adventure" was she proposing?

_____

_____

_____

Are we suggesting you scout out a forest, orchard, or vineyard and plan an outdoor rendezvous with your husband? Not exactly. We are suggesting that God gave you an imagination for a reason. He doesn't intend for intimacy in your marriage to become boring and predictable. Creativity is *you* asking God what intimacy looks like in your unique marriage. It is you thinking outside the box, praying, reading, and waiting on God.

Creativity with Little Ones

When we had three children and the oldest was three, this Mommy was *so* tired and just didn't feel creative. By the time everything was done and it was time for bed, passion was the last thing on my mind. I knew I couldn't put sex on the shelf until the kids were older so I asked God to show me how to get creative and He put this on my mind. Every Saturday when the weather was good, I hired a high school girl to take the kids to a park a few blocks away. With a backpack full of sandwiches, treats, juice, and sweatshirts, the babysitter was instructed to stay away from the house for two to three hours.

I remember the first Saturday this worked. I called Jody into the bedroom and he found me "unclothed." When he asked where the kids were, I said, "*Gone* for two hours. Can you think of any way to spend that time?" Later Jody said, "Wow! To be alone in our own home in the middle of the day when we have energy. Amazing!" I totally agreed.

Creativity with Teens

After adopting an Austrian neighbor (we lived in Vienna as missionaries), we had four teenagers ages 13, 14, 15, and 17. Teens make intimacy difficult as they are curious and never go to bed. So I decided Jody and I should go on hotel dates. With a picnic basket filled with favorite food and drink, a cassette player (shows my age), candles, cards (to play strip poker), and other fun things, I took Jody off to a local hotel from 5:00 p.m. until midnight. Not only was it a time of pursuing passion but a time to talk without the possibility of four teens listening. Jody said it was much more fun than dinner and a movie!

Empty-Nest Creativity

It was Jody's birthday—what could I do that would be fun and passion filled? I went to where our camper was stored and set it up for a party. Balloons, a cake, dinner all prepared plus fun snacks and, of course, gifts. When I did the setup, the weather was nice for January. Five hours later, it was snowing. So we trudged through snow to the camper, laughing, and had a sweet time of dinner, intimacy, and a party in a camper that wasn't exactly warm. So we left early still laughing about my attempt at creative passion in the snow!

As you think about trying something new, think about this cute advice from a long married couple to the question, "What if the new stuff we try isn't as satisfying as our old standbys?"

What do you mean "if"? In most cases, I can promise you it won't be. When you try the floor instead of the bed, you may end up with carpet burns on your knees and a sore back the next morning! If you sneak out in the dead of night to enjoy your lover by the light of the silvery moon, you may both end up with the worst case of chiggers in three counties.

But that isn't the point. You were adventurers! You've made a special memory, even if it turned out to be a hilarious disaster. You stirred up the water of your marriage to keep it from going stagnant. The next day, the following week, five years from now, you'll still be able to chuckle over your little secret, shaking your heads at how crazy you both were to try some of the things you did. When you return to your old favorites, you will appreciate them more.[1]

Below is an adventure I, Juli, planned for Mike. He *really* liked it and I won't tell you what he bought for me to wear!

The Fashion Show Adventure

Take your husband to the mall. Promise him that this will not be like any other trip to the mall. Once you get in the mall, give your husband a budget (or not) and tell him that you are going shopping together. He can pick out any outfit in the entire mall for you to wear when you get home. Whatever he picks out (even if it's a Yankees jersey—*yuck!*), you have to wear it without a negative comment. Have fun!

 4. Talk with your husband about planning a sexual adventure.

 5. Whatever stage you are in—just married, baby, little kids, teens, or empty nest— plan a creative sexual surprise for your husband. (If you need more ideas, consider *Simply Romantic Nights* by Family Life.)

DAY 2

Setting the Stage: The SHM Way

The SHM did more than plan sexual field trips. Both she and Solomon created an atmosphere that said, "Our bedroom is a place to be together sexually. It is our hideaway." Solomon even ordered cedar beams from SHM's home country to be installed in the ceiling of their bridal chamber to make her feel comfortable in the palace (see Song 1:17).

♥ 1. Read SOS 1:16–17. What do you think it means in verse 16 that their "couch" (meaning their bed) was "luxuriant" (NASB)?

_____

_____

_____ ■

♥ 2. Write a paragraph describing your bedroom.

_____

_____

_____

_____ ■

What feeling does your lover receive when he walks into your bedroom? Does the atmosphere speak panic or passion? Does he think he's walked into an office or TV room, laundry folding station or Lover's Hideaway? Tragically, the master bedroom is often the last room to be picked up or decorated. Friend, walk into your bedroom and take a long look. And don't give up and say, "We just don't have the money."

Linda's friend Lorraine turned their master bedroom and bath into an English garden. A bit of floral wallpaper, a sheet made into a dust ruffle with matching curtains, and white lattice nailed to several walls began the new look. Then Lorraine wove silk ivy and twinkle lights through the lattice for a soft atmosphere, added a white garden bench and an English birdcage she bought at a garage sale. Finally, one coat from a can of green spray paint applied to picture frames, lamp shades, and a table completed the transformation. Total cost: three hundred dollars.[2]

I, Juli, painted our bedroom Smokin' Hot red when we needed a change of scenery.

♥ 3. If your bedroom is not a hideaway that invites intimacy, ask God to give you one or two ideas to begin your bedroom transformation. Write the ideas here and do them!

_____

_____

_____

_____ ■

Sexual pleasure is heightened when it involves all the senses: touch, sound, taste, sight, and smell. Smokin' Hot Mama set the stage for lovemaking by involving the senses.

💟 4. Read Song 1:12–13. How did SHM use fragrance in lovemaking?

_____

_____

_____ ∎

If you walked into Solomon and SHM's bedroom, powerful fragrances would overwhelm you. Scented powders were spread over the bed linens and on the satin curtains covering the walls. The bride and groom would also be wearing their personal fragrant lotions designed to delight the other. As one five-year-old boy said, "Love is when a girl puts on perfume and a boy puts on shaving cologne and they go out and smell each other."

Did you know that fragrance affects us in powerful ways? "The quickest way to induce a change in emotions or mood is through smell, because the sense of smell reacts more quickly on the brain than other senses. The top odor for putting men in the mood for love was a combination of pumpkin pie and lavender."[3] We're not sure how you are to combine these two, maybe make a pumpkin pie and spray the room with lavender scent!

💟 5. What can you do to incorporate the five senses into your lovemaking? Talk with your husband about what he would like. Possibly share these ideas with him.

_____

_____

_____ ∎

Scent: Scented candles or sweet smelling flowers. One creative wife dabbed cologne on the lightbulbs. When intimacy time was near, she turned on the lights and allowed the scent to waft through the room.

Sound: Consider a tabletop fountain that sounds like a bubbling brook. Or put sounds of gentle rain, a waterfall, or thunder on your smartphone or iPad.

Touch: Too often after years of marriage, touch becomes a platonic peck on the cheek or deep sexual touch. Consider rediscovering gentle touch. To spice things up, heat baby oil and drop one drop of fragrance in it. Spread an old sheet on the floor or bed and give your lover a hot oil massage. The lovemaking is slippery but fun!

Taste: Your favorite drink on ice. Strawberries, pineapple, blackberries on toothpicks that you feed to each other. Whatever tempts your taste buds is what you get.

Marnie: My husband and I take a jar of Nutella to bed with two spoons. Chocolate puts me in the mood for romance!

Sight: "According to a survey conducted by the National Opinion Research Center at the University of Chicago, the second most appealing sexual act for men and women (preceded only by intercourse) was watching a partner undress."[4] Whether a slow undressing or a swaying dance, God made a husband to be aroused by the sight of his wife's body.

♥ 6. Read Song 7:1– 8. SHM was wearing either a flimsy garment or her skin. Write three sentences to describe Solomon's delight in the sight of his wife.

_____

_____

_____ ∎

Don't write off SHM's dance too quickly! Yes, it's tempting to think, _I'm not displaying my very imperfect body like that!_ We are certainly not suggesting you buy a coconut bra and grass skirt like Juli wore in the DVD study! We are asking you to look honestly at God's Word in the Song and see how free SHM was. You don't have to copy her or anyone. You are God's special creation of you, and He desires to show you what it looks like for _you_ to be free with your body and delight your husband with the sight of you.

DAY 3

Talking like a SHM

Talking about sex is just awkward. What do you say? What words do you use? How do you describe what you like? Some words just seem too crass, others too technical. "Honey, I'm going to turn you on by touching your vagina" just doesn't send romantic chills through most wives. As a result, the average couple simply avoids talking about sex.

What would your finances look like if you never talked about money? How would you parent your children if you and your husband had no way to talk about discipline or expectations for your kids? Communication is key to success in every area—including a great sex life.

So let's turn again to SHM and see how she handled the challenge of communication. The language of love is poetic and Solomon and SHM developed their own sexual, private language. They chose the poetic words _garden_ and _fruit_. These words are warm, imaginative, and erotic. A garden is a lush private place where beautiful flowers bloom. Sometimes a brook flows through the garden. The imagery is beautiful. Fruit looks appetizing and tastes sweet. Most importantly, SHM and her husband knew exactly what each word meant!

♥ 1. Do you and your husband have a "sexual" language? If so, does it need to be expanded?

_____

_____

_____ ∎

♥ 2. Why do you think being able to communicate freely about sexual things is important to improving your sex life?

_____

_____

_____ ■

♥ 3. Take a walk alone with the Lord (or kneel by your couch) and share your fears, insecurities, and just plain discomfort about talking about your body, his body, just anything you feel uncomfortable about in thinking about a private sexual language. You won't embarrass God! Remember He is the One who wrote the words *garden* and *fruit* in the Song.

_____

_____

_____ ■

If you want to become a Smokin' Hot Mama with a smokin' hot sex life, you need to learn to communicate about everything intimate with your husband. You can use the words Solomon and SHM used or be creative and make up your own special names. One wife calls her husband's intimate parts "the Lighthouse on the Rocks." As a gift, he gave her a framed picture of a lighthouse. It sits on the nightstand by their bed, a sweet secret shared by them alone.[5]

One couple who just could not find private names decided to use their middle names, John and Sue. So when the husband would say, "John wants to play with Sue," the wife knows exactly what he is asking!

Part of your sexual vocabulary should also include private code words to communicate the desire to make love. "Well, do you want to do it tonight?" just isn't exciting. Here are some code words couples have used.

Hideaway—"Let's spend time in our secret hideaway."

Sailing—"Let's go sailing." (Translation: "Let's enjoy twenty minutes of loving.") Variations include: "I'd enjoy a speedboat ride." (Think you know the translation?) Or "How about a long luxurious cruise this weekend?" (an hour or more of lovemaking).

A home-cooked meal (translation: twenty minutes of lovemaking). "I'm in the mood for a gourmet feast" (an hour or more of lovemaking). "Let's get fast food tonight" (a quickie).

Some couples use symbols instead of words to say they are interested in lovemaking.

Candles: "We keep two candles in our bedroom. If I light one, my husband knows I'm interested in making love. If he lights the second candle, I know my invite has been accepted. One time, I lit the candle. Later, instead of finding only one other candle lit, I discovered my husband had placed candles all around the room!"[6]

Bunnies: My husband and I have two cute stuffed bunnies, one pink and one blue. If I want to make love, I put the pink bunny on the bed (or hide it in a place I know he will find it). If the blue bunny joins the pink bunny against the pillows on the bed, his answer is "Yes, let's do it!"

Flirting: When my husband wants to tell me that he wants to be intimate, he quickly pulls his zipper up and down. It's his cute way of telling me what's on his mind. (Obviously the kids are not around!)

♥ 4. Find a time alone as a couple; make a list of all the words you can think of for the private areas of both of your bodies. Then write down words or phrases for "making love." Next, you and your husband talk about the words or phrases you like and the ones that make you uncomfortable. Discuss the images you both enjoy (hideaway, sandy beach) and whether that image might be suitable for your private love language.

_____

_____

_____

_____

_____ ■

♥ 5. You and your husband together develop code words or symbols that indicate desire for intimacy.

_____

_____

_____

_____

_____ ■

Here Are Some More Fun Ways to Use Your Private Words in Sweet Sexual Encounters.

Seven Things I Love about Your Body

Examples:

- I love your arms and the way they hold me.
- I love your mouth and the way it compliments me.
- I love your _____ and the way it pleasures me.

Write out the seven things you love about his body and give it to him at a special private dinner. Then show him how you love these seven things about his body! (Consider getting brave and sharing something you like that you haven't told him before.) And, of course, he can play the game too and write out the seven things he loves about your body!

Rewrite the Rules

Choose any word game, such as Scrabble, Boggle, etc. Play as normal but use only words that are related to love, sex, and romance. Before you begin, make up your own rules for what one must do if he or she cannot make a word and must pass. And decide what the "prize" will be for the winner!

Alphabet Love

This game is like kindergarten—but for big people. The husband initiates by kissing any part of his wife's body that begins with "A" (such as ankle). She reciprocates by kissing any part of his body that starts with "B." Continue alternating through Z. You'll be surprised how motivated your spouse will be to conjure up adjectives and anatomical descriptions you've never heard before!

DAY 4
The Extravagant Love of SHM

Are you beginning to understand SHM? She loves extravagantly. She loves erotically. She builds her husband up and delights him with her sexual abandonment. She is free with her words and with her body.

You have seen passion bursting forth from Song of Solomon. This week you've studied about SHM's creative passion, the passion of her words and how she set the stage for intimacy. You've learned much about her sexual love for Solomon and how she enticed him with private sexual words and erotic actions.

We hope, like us, that your heart has been opened to the beauty and joy of sexual love as you've seen a glimpse of SHM's heart. As we close this last chapter of *Passion Pursuit*, we want you to see more fully how Smokin' Hot Mama became so "Smokin' Hot."

The world gives us many examples of smokin' hot romances that quickly fade away after the challenges of life and selfishness hit. Beautiful bodies, million-dollar bedrooms, and extravagant vacations aren't enough to sustain a smokin' hot love through the normal trials of marriage. Toward the end of Song of Solomon, there are two little verses that are packed with the secret beauty of a love that endures. In these verses, SHM reveals the powerful picture of the source of her sexual love. These short verses are perhaps the most memorable and intense of the Song. Some have even declared them one of the most beautiful pictures of love ever written, revealing a love that is intimate, intense, indestructible, and invaluable.

♥ 1. Read Song 8:6–7. Write it here.

_____

_____

_____

_____

_____

_____

_____ ■

In these verses, we see three qualities of marital love that make it absolutely invaluable. SHM speaks of a love so wide, so high, and so deep that it is impossible to describe. She uses a series of images to try to express the depth of her love for Solomon. Let's look at her description, image by image.

Love Is Intimate

"Place me like a seal over your heart, like a seal on your arm." (verse 6)

Today you wear a wedding ring, which says, _I am one with my husband._ In the SHM's time, a seal on the arm signified the same thing. It meant, "I belong to this man. He belongs to me." Their love was all about them and only them. Their sexual intimacy was an expression of belonging completely to each other.

Love Is Intense

"For love is as strong as death, its jealousy unyielding as the grave." (verse 6)

Speaking of death and love together? It doesn't sound very romantic. Perhaps SHM was saying, _Like death, our love is permanent and irreversible. Its endurance is as strong as death._ The use of the word _jealous_ speaks of single-minded devotion.

"Its flashes are flashes of fire, the very flame of the Lord." (verse 6, our translation)

The image of a hotly burning flame reveals the power and energy of the love between husband and wife. It is a holy and beautiful picture. Its flashes are the very flame of the Lord. What are the flashes? Of course, the sparks of sexual passion are there but the intensity of the passion comes from the companionship, the servant love, sacrifice, loyalty, and commitment. This is not the momentary excitement of "hooking up" or an affair but the sexual explosion found only in lifelong love.

Love Is Indestructible

"Many waters cannot quench love; rivers cannot wash it away." (verse 7)

A flame can usually be extinguished with water but not a flame ignited by the Lord God Almighty because it is fueled by the energy of God Himself. In effect, she is saying that no matter what challenges come our way, our love will last because it is built upon holy love.

Think of these qualities as the three essential elements of genuine, romantic love: intimate, intense, and indestructible. Often, the world speaks of passionate love that has one or maybe two of these qualities. But the trifecta of intimate oneness, fiery passion, and lifelong commitment is a priceless treasure.

"If a man were to give all the riches of his house for love, it would be utterly despised." (verse 7 NASB)

If you won the lottery or inherited a vast amount of wealth, it would not be enough to purchase this powerful flame of love whose flashes are the lightning bolts of God Himself.

2. Now that you understand these two beautiful verses about love a little better, write your own paraphrase of them here.

A beautiful paraphrase follows:

"O my Beloved, press me close to your heart. Wrap me in your arms and hold me tight as your most precious possession. Your love, strong as death, seizes me with an irresistible force. I give myself to this love and yearn to be wholly and completely absorbed by it. My love for you is violent, vigorous, unceasing. I could no more give you up than the grave would give up the dead. My passionate love is a flame not kindled by man but by the Holy God. It is a waterproof torch, a flame of fire that mighty waters cannot quench."[7]

One of the challenges of learning from SHM is that her life might seem to be nothing like yours. She was married to a king thousands of years ago. However, sexual love as God designed it hasn't changed. Just as she longed for a love that was fiery and indestructible, we know women who make this a twenty-first-century reality. Here's one modern example of this kind of lifelong love, written from the perspective of a daughter:

Last weekend, we celebrated my parents' fiftieth wedding anniversary. This morning they left on a long-awaited trip to Hawaii. They were as excited as if it were their honeymoon. When my parents married, they had only enough money for a three-day trip fifty miles from home. At that time, they made a pact that each time they made love, they would put a dollar in a special metal box and save it for a honeymoon in Hawaii for their fiftieth anniversary. Dad was a policeman and Mom was a schoolteacher. They lived in a modest house and did all their own repairs. Raising five children was a challenge, and sometimes money was short. But no matter what emergency came up, Dad would not let Mom take any money out of the "Hawaii account." As the account grew, they put it in a savings account.

My parents were always very much in love. I can remember Dad's coming home and telling Mom, "I have a dollar in my pocket," and she would smile at him and reply, "I know how to spend it." When each of us children married, Mom and Dad gave us a small metal box and told us their secret, which we found enchanting. All five of us are now saving for our dream honeymoons. Mom and Dad never told us how much money they had managed to save but it must have been considerable because, when they cashed in those accounts, they had enough for airfare to Hawaii plus hotel accommodations for ten days and plenty of spending money. As they told us goodbye before leaving, Dad winked and said, "Tonight, we are starting an account for Cancun. That should only take twenty-five years!"[8]

♥ 3. Write a paragraph describing what the five children learned about a passionate lifelong intimacy from their parents.

_____

_____

_____

_____

_____

_____

_____

_____

♥ 4. Thinking of the three qualities of love expressed in Song of Solomon (intimate, intense, and indestructible), how would you describe these three aspects of your sexual love?

_____

_____

_____ ■

From the beginning of *Passion Pursuit*, we have taught you that God's picture of sexual love between a husband and wife is holy and hot. It is consuming and beautiful. Its flashes are the very flashes of the Lord. He, your great God, is the center of all love, including your sexual love.

DAY 5

The Secret Place: Expressing Love to the Lord

The Bible is very clear that sexual intimacy is a metaphor for intimacy with Christ. In chapter 3, you learned that the word for sexual intimacy, *yada*, is also the word used for knowing the Lord.

♥ 1. To refresh your memory, read Ephesians 5:31–32. What does this passage state about the correlation between marital intimacy and spiritual intimacy with the Lord?

_____

_____

_____ ■

This week, we have encouraged you to become creative and uninhibited in your expression of sexual love. God also desires that you become creative and abandoned in your love for Him. In fact, we believe there is some correlation between growing in these two areas. Just as you are learning about freedom in expressing sexual love, you are also on a journey to discover the joy of knowing and loving the Lord. This is how Bethany felt:

I have just realized that I just need to "do it" to deepen my relationship with the Lord. I need to prayerfully spend a good amount of time in His Word and humbly ask Him to teach me how to worship. I think the best time to do this will be in the morning before my eight-month-old wakes up. I just need to do it and I know the Lord will meet me there!

To deepen my relationship with my husband, I also need to prayerfully approach him in creative ways to increase our sex life. I need to give myself permission to be a godly but sensuous wife for him. I just need to put forth the time and effort to plan time together so I can SHOW him how much he means to me! If I do this, I know it will be blessed.

On both of these accounts, I know my time and efforts will be blessed and it will be well worth my time, for the short-term and long-term.

Of all the characters we learn about in the Bible, King David (Solomon's father) was the one who stands out as a man who knew how to be intimate with the Lord. He used his creativity, language, his mind, and his body to express love to the Lord. Many of David's psalms speak of his intense desire to know the Lord's presence and to express his love in worship.

♥ 2. Read Psalm 63:1–8 and Psalm 42:1–2. Describe the longing David expresses in these psalms.

_____

_____

_____ ∎

David was also expressive in his effusive praise of the Lord. Just as SHM and her husband continually speak of the beauty of their lover, David's psalms constantly strive to proclaim the beauty of his Lord.

♥ 2. Read Psalm 57:7–11 and Psalm 100:1–5. How do these expressions of love parallel the type of language used in the SOS?

_____

_____

_____ ∎

♥ 3. Read 2 Samuel 6:14–22. Describe how David worshiped the Lord.

_____

_____

_____ ∎

♥ 4. What do you think David meant when he said, "I will celebrate before the Lord. I will become even more undignified than this, and I will be humiliated in my own eyes"?

_____

_____

_____ ■

♥ 5. What keeps you from expressing your love for the Lord with abandonment?

_____

_____

_____ ■

May We Speak a Blessing Over You?

Even though we have probably never met you, we have become your friends over the past ten weeks. We have prayed for you and sought the Lord for His words to touch your heart. We long for the mighty God to revolutionize intimacy in your marriage! We look forward to hearing stories about how He has brought healing, pleasure, forgiveness, and beauty. However, we have a greater prayer for you . . . that you find deep intimacy with the Lord Jesus Christ. We pray that He shows you how physical intimacy and the lifelong

commitment of marriage is only a shadow of His great love for you. We pray that He awakens your heart to seek Him and worship Him as David did.

Even the best marriage someday will end. The greatest lovers will be separated as time presses on. However, your intimate relationship with the Lord will continue from everlasting to everlasting. Be consumed by Him in longing and worship!

Behold, I am coming soon! My reward is with me, and I will give to everyone according to what he has done. I am the Alpha and the Omega, the First and the Last, the Beginning and the End.

The Spirit and the bride say, "Come!" And let him who hears say, "Come!" Whoever is thirsty, let him come; and whoever wishes, let him take the free gift of the water of life. (Revelation 22:12, 17)

NOTES

Chapter 1: I've Got Power

1. Dr. Julianna Slattery, *Finding the Hero in Your Husband* (Deerfield Beach, FL: Health Communications, Inc., 2001), xvii.
2. Ibid., 9.
3. David Mindoff, *Oy Vey: More!* (New York: HarperCollins, 2001), 6.
4. Linda Dillow, *What's It Like to Be Married to Me?* (Colorado Springs: David C Cook, 2011), 77.

Chapter 2: Me, Pursue Passion?

1. Dr. Joseph and Linda Dillow, Dr. Peter and Lorraine Pintus, *Intimacy Ignited* (Colorado Springs: NavPress, 2004), 15.
2. Ibid., 10.
3. *Ryrie Study Bible*, Song of Solomon 5:1b says, "God then speaks and blesses the union."
4. Dr. Howard Hendricks, in a telephone conversation with Linda Dillow.

Chapter 3: God's Got an Opinion!

1. Philip Yancey, "Holy Sex," *Christianity Today*, October 2003, 48–49.
2. Ruth Smythers, "Instruction and Advice for the Young Bride," *The Madison Institute Newsletter* (New York: Spiritual Guidance Press, fall 1894).
3. C. S. Lewis, *Mere Christianity* (San Francisco: Harper, 2001), 98.
4. Mike Mason, *The Mystery of Marriage* (Portland, OR: Multnomah, 2005), 132.
5. John Piper, *This Momentary Marriage* (Wheaton, IL: Crossway, 2012), 135.
6. Linda Dillow and Lorraine Pintus, *Intimate Issues* (Colorado Springs: WaterBrook Press, 1999), 25.
7. Mason, *The Mystery of Marriage*, 136.
8. John Piper, ed. *Sex and the Supremacy of Christ* (Wheaton, IL: Crossway, 2005), 26.
9. Clifford and Joyce Penner, *The Gift of Sex* (Nashville: Thomas Nelson, 2003), 40.
10. Gary Thomas, *Sacred Marriage* (Grand Rapids: Zondervan, 2000), 226.

Chapter 4: Making Truth Stick

1. Francis Frangipane, *The Three Battlegrounds* (Cedar Rapids, IA: Arrow Publications, 1989), 25.
2. Ibid., 28.
3. Ibid., 77.
4. Paul E. Billheimer, *Destined for the Throne* (Minneapolis: Bethany House, 1975), 120–121.

Chapter 5: What Kind of Love Are You Making?

1. Juli Slattery, *No More Headaches* (Carol Stream, IL: Tyndale, 2009), 96.
2. Sally Meredith, in a private paper given to Linda Dillow.

Chapter 6: Pursuing Pure Pleasure

1. W. F. Arndt and E. W. Gingrich, *A Greek-English Lexicon of the New Testament* (Grand Rapids: Zondervan, 1957), s.v. "molvno" (impure).
2. Bromley, *The International Standard Bible Encyclopedia*. s.v. "crime."

3. *The Lexicon Webster Dictionary*, vol. 2, s.v. "sodomy."

4. Bromley, *The International Standard Bible Encyclopedia*, s.v. "sodomite."

5. R. Laird Harris, Gleason Archer, Bruce Waltke, *Theological Wordbook of the Old Testament*, vol. 2 (Chicago: Moody, 1980), s.v. "gadesh."

6. Dr. Lewis Smedes, *Sex for Christians* (Grand Rapids: Eerdmans, 1976, 1994), 212.

7. Ryrie Study Bible (Chicago: Moody), note on Proverbs 1:2.

Chapter 7: Exposing Counterfeit Intimacy

1. Oswald Chambers, *My Utmost for His Highest* (Grand Rapids: Discovery House, 1992), April 19.

2. Juli Slattery, *No More Headaches* (Carol Stream, IL: Tyndale, 2009), 179–82.

Chapter 8: Debt-Free Intimacy

1. The standard Greek lexicon translates it "count, take into account," Frederick W. Danker and Walter Bauer, *A Greek-English Lexicon of the New Testament and Other Early Christian Literature,* 3rd ed. (Chicago: University of Chicago Press, 2000), 597.

2. R. T. Kendall, *Total Forgiveness* (Lake Mary, FL: Charisma House, 2002), 149.

3. Clara Barton, cited by Luis Palau in the message "Experiencing God's Forgiveness."

4. Allen T. Edmunds, *Reader's Digest*, January 1982, 90.

5. Stormie Omartian, *The Power of a Praying Wife* (Eugene, OR: Harvest House, 1997), 2.

Chapter 9: The Passion Priority

1. Douglas E. Rosenau, *A Celebration of Sex* (Nashville: Thomas Nelson, 1994), 85.

2. Ibid., 86.

3. My thanks to author and speaker Cynthia Heald for this powerful comment that has so influenced my life. (Linda)

4. Dan B. Allender and Tremper Longman III, *Intimate Allies* (Wheaton, IL: Tyndale, 1999), 233–34.

5. Ron Allen, *Worship, The Missing Jewel of the Christian Church* (Portland, OR.: Multnomah, 1982), 120.

6. Juli Slattery, *No More Headaches* (Carol Stream, IL: Tyndale, 2009), 144.

7. John F. Walvoord and Roy B. Zuck, *Bible Knowledge Commentary* (Wheaton: Victor Books, 1983), 517.

8. John Mitchell quote from Ruth Myers, *Treasury of Praise* (Sisters, OR: Multnomah, 2007), 3.

9. Merlin Carothers, *Prison to Praise* (Escondido, CA: Merlin R. Carothers, 1970), 85.

Chapter 10: Becoming a Smokin' Hot Mama

1. Stephen and Judith Schwambach, *For Lovers Only* (Eugene, OR: Harvest House, 1990), 198.

2. Linda Dillow and Lorraine Pintus, *Intimate Issues* (Colorado Springs: WaterBrook Press, 1999), 223.

3. Alan R. Hirsch, M.D., in *How to Romance the Man You Love*, by the editors of Prevention Magazine health books (Emmaus, PA: Rodale Press, 1997), 34.

4. *University of Chicago Chronicle* Oct. 13, 1994. Vol. 14 no. 4.

5. Dr. Joseph and Linda Dillow, Dr. Peter and Lorraine Pintus, *Intimacy Ignited* (Colorado Springs: NavPress, 2004), 73.

6. Ibid., 74.

7. Ibid., 220.

8. Ann Landers, *Colorado Springs Gazette*, June 6, 1998, Lifestyle, 5.

Acknowledgments

We thank our great God for the privilege of partnering with the Holy Spirit and with each other to write *Passion Pursuit*.

Our husbands are our greatest encouragers. Thank you, Mike and Jody, for praying for us, for understanding when our minds were preoccupied, and for encouraging us when writing was hard. We are so grateful to God for you!

To Terry Behimer, director of all Authentic Intimacy writing projects and our editor who makes us sound good. You are so wonderful to work with and we are *so* grateful to God for you, our dear friend and coworker.

To Deana Williams, our dear friend and coworker who did everything for the DVD taping and the website. You are amazing and we are so thankful for you!

To two incredible women's ministry directors, Donna Graham and Lynda Rosenhahn of Rocky Mountain Calvary in Colorado Springs. Teaching the pilot of *Passion Pursuit* at RMC was a joy! Partnering with you was a delight. You have encouraged us every step of the way and we are incredibly thankful to you both.

To our wonderful small group leaders at Rocky Mountain Calvary: Lynda Rosenhahn, Tracy Swionteck, Lorna Bennett, Lisa Beech, Michele Davis, Sandy Brown, Kim Hooker, and Leah Green. You cheered us on every week and we are grateful for each of you.

To the sixty brave women at Rocky Mountain Calvary who were our "guinea pigs" during the pilot study of *Passion Pursuit*.

To Holly Kisly and Rene' Hanebutt, our Moody Publishers Authentic Intimacy team. What a joy it is to partner with you in bringing God's truth to His precious women! We thank God for your hearts and your expertise in bringing *Passion Pursuit* to life!

To our many friends who supported us with prayer and encouragement on this journey. We are especially grateful to Lorraine Pintus. Lorraine, your unwavering support for this project and consistent prayer has been a tremendous blessing to both of us.

Discussion Guidelines

You may choose to go through this Bible study alone or share it with a friend or small group. We think community can bring encouragement and great discussion. However, talking about such an intimate topic can be tricky! Here are a few guidelines that will keep discussions throughout *Passion Pursuit* honoring to God and to your husband:

1. Under no circumstances should you share with others intimate details about your sexual relationship with your husband. No one should ever be able to visualize you and your husband in bed. It would be wise to reassure your husband of your commitment to keep your sexual relationship private.

2. All discussions are to be kept confidential.

3. No negative or embarrassing comments about husbands are allowed.

4. Keep your focus on what changes *you* need to make, not on those your husband needs to make.

5. No one will be asked to talk about anything that makes her feel uncomfortable.

AUTHENTIC INTIMACY

HOW DO I FIND OUT MORE?

Where can Christian women go to ask their most private questions about sex? Authentic Intimacy is that place (www.authenticintimacy.com). In a bold, honest, and safe setting, you'll discover biblical answers, practical help, and lasting hope in this most personal area of your life. Are you curious about what God thinks is okay in the bedroom? Do you regret some choices you made in the past? God is ready to shine light into your deepest and most significant areas of need. Authentic Intimacy is building a community of women who want to be truthful about their journey, their struggles, and their questions about life's most significant issues.

WAYS TO GET INVOLVED

Authentic Intimacy is a community that needs you.

Here are simple ways to get involved.

- Follow us on Facebook and Twitter

- Interact with our blogs and forums, giving us feedback and sharing your story.

- If you like what we are doing, tell your friends!

---

www.authenticintimacy.com